YOU AND YOUR PENSION

YOU AND YOUR PENSION

Published by Consumers' Association
and Hodder & Stoughton

Which? Books are commissioned and researched by
The Association for Consumer Research and
published by Consumers' Association,
2 Marylebone Road, London NW1 4DX and
Hodder & Stoughton, 47 Bedford Square, London WC1B 3DP

Researched and written by Jonquil Lowe
Typographic design by Paul Saunders
Cover artwork by Larry Rostant

First edition May 1990

Copyright © 1990 Consumers' Association Ltd

British Library Cataloguing in Publication Data
You and your pension
   1. Great Britain. Superannuation schemes
   I. Title   II. Consumers' Association
   331. 2520941

ISBN 0 340 50373 4

Photoset by Paston Press, Loddon, Norfolk
Printed and bound in Great Britain by Collins, Glasgow

CONTENTS

INTRODUCTION

There are many demands on your money, especially in the earlier years of life when you may be buying your own home, or raising a family. It's tempting to forget about saving for retirement – not because it's unimportant, but because all the other demands are so much more pressing. Retirement, however, is an increasingly long and important stage of life and, if you want it to be comfortable, you need to build up substantial savings during your working years. Delaying the start of retirement saving means you'll have to save a lot extra once you do start. And delaying too long could mean that you have to settle for a much lower retirement income than you would wish.

The government encourages you to save for your retirement by giving favourable tax treatment to most specialised pension schemes and plans. Unfortunately, the many changes to rules about pensions have made the whole area ridiculously complex. It's difficult enough sorting out the choices you face, let alone which option is the best.

This book will put you on the right course and help you to plan sensibly. It looks at the methods you can choose for retirement saving, and guides you through the choices that apply to you. This book is aimed partly at those people who are still some way from retirement and have time to plan ahead. But it also includes guidance on boosting your pension – even late on in your working life – and takes you through the steps for claiming your pensions once you decide the time has come to ease up on work and to set out on what may be the most pleasant stage of your life.

=1=

YOUR RETIREMENT INCOME

Leisure at last

Thanks to advances in medicine, better diet and housing, and improved working conditions, you can expect to live to a ripe old age. Also, increased affluence means that many people can now choose when they want to retire rather than soldiering on until the state pension age. Retirement is no longer made up of a few twilight years but is a phase of life which can easily last two or even three decades.

Table 1: Average length of retirement

If you retire at age:	you can expect this many years in retirement:	
	women	*men*
50	30	25
55	25	21
60	21	17
65	17	13
70	14	10

Source: Government Actuary's Department

Retirement is becoming a long and welcome phase of life in which you have leisure at last to pursue your hobbies, indulge your interests, return to earlier studies or maybe even adopt a new career.

How much retirement income?

To make the most of retirement you need to have sufficient income. You're looking a long way ahead, so you'll have to estimate how much income would be enough. Your estimate will be based on your likely *needs* in retirement and the type of lifestyle you *want*. Your income needs may be less in retirement than now if, say, you'll have paid off a mortgage, can save on travel to work, or will need one car in the family instead of two. On the other hand, needs could rise if, say, you have to replace a car previously provided by your employer, or pay for meals that had been cheap, or free, at work. In later retirement, you may need more income because of higher spending on health care – you might decide to set aside savings in early retirement to cope with this or consider taking out insurance to cover medical bills.

You may want to spend more on your lifestyle once you retire: you might want to take up hobbies for which you didn't previously have time; you might want to travel more. If you travel a lot already, your spending might fall in retirement because you're likely to have the flexibility to travel at cheaper times.

You can fill in the Expense Calculator on pp. 12 and 13 to give you a guide to your expected retirement spending. Write down your estimates in *today's* prices and values. The total gives you an idea – in today's money – of the after-tax retirement income that you'll want. In general, you'll need a lower *before-tax* income than now to finance your chosen lifestyle because older people qualify for higher tax-free allowances (see Chapter 14). But, if you decide to retire relatively early, this won't apply for the first few years.

Don't ignore inflation

It's not easy deciding how much you need to set aside for retirement. The problem is made more difficult because of the effect of inflation. Rising prices erode the buying power of your money. Chart 1 below shows what inflation can do to the prices of everyday items:

Chart 1: Inflation in your shopping basket

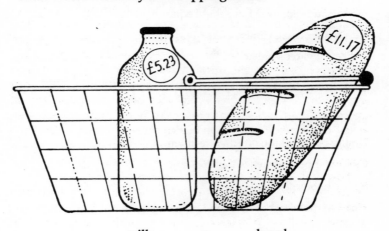

	milk		bread	
	1990 price	30p	1990 price	64p
yearly inflation:	**5%**	**10%**	**5%**	**10%**
year				
2000	£0.48	£0.78	£1.04	£1.66
2010	£0.80	£2.02	£1.70	£4.31
2020	£1.30	£5.23	£2.77	£11.17

Inflation means that in future you'll need more £££ of income just to maintain the *same* standard of living as now. For example, five per cent a year inflation means that, in 20 years' time, you need an income of over £26,000 to be able to buy the same amount that you can buy now with £10,000. Put another way, a yearly income of £10,000 today would then be worth only the same as £3,750 now, in terms of what it could buy 20 years' ahead.

11

Expense Calculator

Living at home   *yearly total*

Food shopping and household basics   £_____

Buying and repairing household equipment   £_____

Newspapers/magazines/books   £_____

TV licence/videos/music   £_____

Dog/cat/other pets   £_____

Living it up

Dining out/drinking out/theatre/cinema   £_____

Clothes/shoes/cosmetics/hairdressing   £_____

Sports/hobbies/clubs   £_____

Holidays/holiday home/second home   £_____

Car

Owning: tax/insurance/servicing/repairs/
        breakdown service   £_____

Renting: rental charge   £_____

Running: petrol/oil/parking   £_____

House

Mortgage/rent/service charge   £_____

Repairs/improvements/decoration/furnishing   £_____

Buildings and contents insurance   £_____

Community charge/water rates   £_____

Gas/electricity/heating oil/solid fuel   £_____

Home help/window cleaner/other paid help £_____

Garden £_____

Health

Medicine/medical insurance/dentist/optician £_____

Indulgences

Drinking/smoking/betting/pools £_____

Caring

Spending on children/grandchildren £_____

Financial help for elderly relatives £_____

Presents/gifts to charity, church, etc £_____

Protection-only life insurance £_____

Saving

Saving to replace car, household equipment, etc £_____

Saving to cover higher health charges later on £_____

Other saving £_____

Other

Travel/telephone/postage/stationery £_____

Loan repayments (other than mortgage) £_____

Other £_____

TOTAL £_____

Inflation affects both your savings for retirement and your income once you've retired. You need to invest your savings *now* so that they'll stand a good chance of beating inflation, and you need to make sure that once your retirement income starts it will keep pace with inflation. But this isn't so easy, because you don't know what the future rate of inflation will be. Table 2 below shows how different rates of inflation would affect the buying power of your money. For example, if inflation averaged four per cent a year for the next 35 years, the buying power of £1,000 would have been reduced to just £253. That seems bad enough, but if inflation averaged a much higher rate of 10 per cent a year, your £1,000 would be worth just £36 in terms of what it could buy.

Table 2: How inflation could eat into your income

What £1,000 would be worth in future given different rates of inflation

Years	Average yearly rate of inflation						
	4%	5%	6%	7%	8%	9%	10%
	£	£	£	£	£	£	£
1	962	952	943	935	926	917	909
2	925	907	890	873	857	842	826
3	889	864	840	816	794	772	751
4	855	823	792	763	735	708	683
5	822	784	747	713	681	650	621
10	676	614	558	508	463	422	386
15	555	481	417	362	315	275	239
20	456	377	312	258	215	178	149
25	375	295	233	184	146	116	92
30	308	231	174	131	99	75	57
35	253	181	130	94	68	49	36
40	208	142	97	67	46	32	22
45	171	111	73	48	31	21	14
50	141	87	54	34	21	13	9
60	95	53	30	17	10	6	3

Table 3 below looks at inflation from the other angle, and shows how many £££ you'll need in future to have the same buying power as £1,000 today, given different rates of inflation. You can use the second Table to convert the total in your Expense Calculator into the amount of £££, in terms of future price levels, that you expect to need when you retire – see the example overleaf.

Table 3: How many £££ you might need in future

How much money you'd need in future, given different rates of inflation, for it to be worth the same as £1,000 today

Years	Average yearly rate of inflation						
	4%	5%	6%	7%	8%	9%	10%
	£	£	£	£	£	£	£
1	1,040	1,050	1,060	1,070	1,080	1,090	1,100
2	1,082	1,103	1,124	1,145	1,166	1,188	1,210
3	1,125	1,158	1,191	1,225	1,260	1,295	1,331
4	1,170	1,216	1,263	1,311	1,361	1,412	1,464
5	1,217	1,276	1,338	1,403	1,469	1,539	1,611
6	1,265	1,340	1,419	1,501	1,587	1,677	1,772
7	1,316	1,407	1,504	1,606	1,714	1,828	1,949
8	1,369	1,478	1,594	1,718	1,851	1,993	2,144
9	1,423	1,551	1,690	1,839	1,999	2,172	2,358
10	1,480	1,629	1,791	1,967	2,159	2,367	2,594
15	1,801	2,079	2,397	2,759	3,172	3,643	4,177
20	2,191	2,653	3,207	3,870	4,661	5,604	6,728
25	2,666	3,386	4,292	5,427	6,848	8,623	10,835
30	3,243	4,322	5,743	7,612	10,063	13,268	17,449
35	3,946	5,516	7,686	10,677	14,785	20,414	28,102
40	4,801	7,040	10,286	14,974	21,725	31,409	45,259
45	5,841	8,985	13,765	21,002	31,920	48,327	72,890
50	7,107	11,467	18,420	29,457	46,902	74,358	117,391
60	10,520	18,679	32,988	57,946	101,257	176,031	304,482

EXAMPLE

Jack, who's 35 now, would like to retire in the year 2020 at age 65 with an income equivalent to £15,000 a year in terms of today's (1990) money. If inflation averaged five per cent a year in the intervening 30 years, his income would need to be £64,800 a yèar in terms of 2020 money. (If you use the table on the previous page, find the figure in the 5% column and the 30-year row – i.e. £4,322. Multiplying this by 15 gives £64,830.) If inflation averaged 10 per cent a year, Jack's yearly income would need to start at £261,700 in 2020 money.

Sources of retirement income?

There are four main soures of retirement income: pensions from the state, private pensions, income from investments and work you continue to do after retirement. Over half of all pensioners rely mainly on the state for their retirement income, and they make up many of the poorest pensioners. On their own, state pensions just don't provide enough to maintain a reasonable lifestyle. It's important to have other sources of retirement income too.

Table 4: Pensioners' incomes

Before-tax weekly income	Percentage of all pensioner households	
	income from all sources	income mainly from state pensions and benefits
less than £45	15	15
£45 to £59.99	15	14
£60 to £99.99	33	20
£100 to £199.99	25	4
£200 and over	12	0
TOTAL	100%	53%

Source: Family Expenditure Survey 1987

At present, the *average* pensioner household has an income of only £131 a week. About half of this comes from the state. An important way in which you can increase your expected retirement income is by building up your own retirement savings.

Chart 2: Where the money comes from

Each £1 of an average pensioners' income is made up of:

state pensions   43p
private pensions   20p
investments*   22p
work and other   14p

* includes equivalent of rent for owner-occupied homes

Source: Family Expenditure Survey 1987

Building up your own pension

For most people, the best way of saving for retirement is using a specialised pension scheme or plan, since these benefit from several tax advantages:

- you get tax relief up to your highest rate of income tax on the amount you pay into a pension scheme or plan. For example, if you're a basic rate taxpayer, paying £100 into a

plan would cost you only £75, assuming a basic tax rate of 25 per cent
- your retirement savings build up free of any tax on income and capital gains
- when you eventually come to take your pension it's taxable in the same way as your salary or wages have been, but you can usually swap part of the pension for a tax-free lump sum.

The snag with pension savings is that you can't draw them out before retirement, even in an emergency, though with many plans you can borrow on the strength of your retirement savings. In general, this means you need to be absolutely sure that money you set aside for retirement can be committed to long-term saving. On the other hand, you should be wary of putting off saving for retirement. Though other demands may seem more pressing, delaying, even for a few years, dramatically increases the amount of money you need to set aside. This is because the money you invest early has a long time to grow and makes a proportionately greater contribution towards your eventual pension than the money you invest later on. The example below shows how even a small delay can affect the amount you need to save.

EXAMPLE

Jack, who's 35 wants to retire at 65 on an income equivalent to £15,000 a year in today's money. If he provided all this himself, he'd need to save up a cash fund by retirement of about £143,000, in terms of today's money. He'd have a good chance of building that up if he either invested a lump sum of £44,000 now, or saved about £2,450 a year, in today's money, from now until retirement. If he puts off saving for retirement, in five years' time he'll need to invest a lump sum of £54,000 or save £3,300 a year until retirement (in today's money) if he's to meet his retirement income goal.

=2=

YOUR PENSION CHOICES

Here, we give a broad picture of the basic pension choices and guide you to the relevant chapters for details. Once you're familiar with the basics, you can go on to consider other aspects of your pension arrangements, such as what happens when you change jobs, what if you want to retire early, and so on. And pension schemes and plans usually provide benefits other than just a retirement pension for yourself – for example, life insurance and pensions for your widow or widower and children. These other aspects are covered in later chapters. In Chapter 15, we return to your main pension choices to summarise the factors you'll want to take into account in making your decisions.

Your most important sources of retirement income are likely to be a state pension and pensions that you build up privately. Nearly everyone who works builds up some **state basic pension**. If you're an employee, you can also build up **State Earnings Related Pension Scheme (SERPS) pension**, though you can opt out of this provided you have an alternative private pension arrangement. As long as you have earnings, you can build up your own pension too, either through an **employer's pension scheme** or a **personal pension plan**. The particular choices that are open to you depend largely on whether you work for someone else or for yourself. Even if you're not currently working there are steps you may be able to take to protect your pension position.

If you work for an employer

Your employer may run a pension scheme for which you're eligible. You can choose whether or not to join it and, if you already belong, you can leave if you like. Some employers' schemes don't let you join if you're over a certain age, and some may put restrictions on you rejoining later on if you've chosen to leave – different schemes have different rules.

If you leave your employer's scheme or you decide not to join it, or your employer doesn't run a scheme, you can – and, in most cases, should – make your own pension arrangements using a personal pension plan.

As an employee, you're covered by SERPS. If you join or already belong to an employer's pension scheme, you may automatically be opted out of SERPS – in the jargon, you're **contracted out**. If this isn't the case, you can choose whether or not to contract out using a personal pension plan.

Chart 3 on pp. 22 and 23 summarises your pension choices.

If you work for yourself

If you run your own business, you'll *have* to make your own private pension arrangements. If you're self-employed, you can do this using a personal pension plan. If your business is set up as a company, you have more choice: you could take out a personal pension plan but, instead, you could set up your own employer's pension scheme. There are special **executive schemes** and **small self-administered schemes** which can be particularly useful for small companies.

If you're self-employed, you're not eligible for SERPS, so you can build up only a basic pension from the state – it's particularly important that you consider making your own savings for retirement. If you're a director of your own company, you count as an employee, so you're covered by SERPS and you have the same choice about contracting out as any employee – see Chart 3.

Chart 4 on pp. 24 and 25 summarises your pension choices.

If you're not working

If you're not currently employed, your pension choices are limited. However, you should check your position with regard to the state pension – you may still be building up basic pension and, if not, you may be able to make sure that you do. You may also have scope to build up your own personal pension, if you've been earning during the last six years.

Chart 5 on pp. 26 and 27 indicates the action you should take to check your position and summarises the pension choices that may be open to you – at least in theory. In practice, your individual circumstances will be a vital factor in deciding what action you can take.

Chart 3: Pension choices if you work for an employer

YOUR OWN PENSION

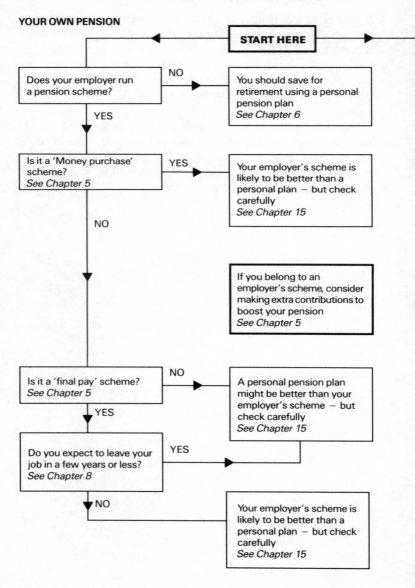

START HERE

Does your employer run a pension scheme?

NO → You should save for retirement using a personal pension plan
See Chapter 6

YES ↓

Is it a 'Money purchase' scheme?
See Chapter 5

YES → Your employer's scheme is likely to be better than a personal plan – but check carefully
See Chapter 15

NO ↓

If you belong to an employer's scheme, consider making extra contributions to boost your pension
See Chapter 5

Is it a 'final pay' scheme?
See Chapter 5

NO → A personal pension plan might be better than your employer's scheme – but check carefully
See Chapter 15

YES ↓

Do you expect to leave your job in a few years or less?
See Chapter 8

YES →

NO ↓

Your employer's scheme is likely to be better than a personal plan – but check carefully
See Chapter 15

YOUR STATE PENSION

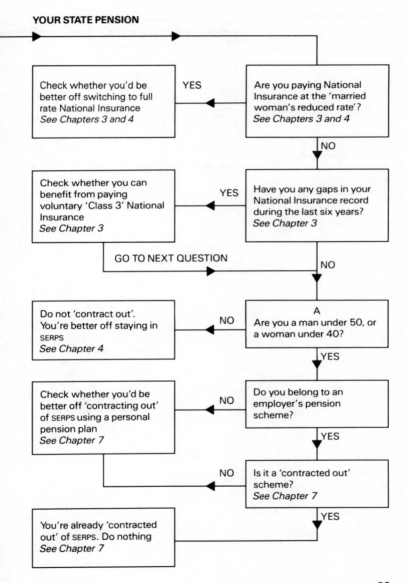

Check whether you'd be better off switching to full rate National Insurance
See Chapters 3 and 4

YES ←

Are you paying National Insurance at the 'married woman's reduced rate'?
See Chapters 3 and 4

NO ↓

Check whether you can benefit from paying voluntary 'Class 3' National Insurance
See Chapter 3

YES ←

Have you any gaps in your National Insurance record during the last six years?
See Chapter 3

GO TO NEXT QUESTION →

NO ↓

Do not 'contract out'. You're better off staying in SERPS
See Chapter 4

NO ←

A
Are you a man under 50, or a woman under 40?

YES ↓

Check whether you'd be better off 'contracting out' of SERPS using a personal pension plan
See Chapter 7

NO ←

Do you belong to an employer's pension scheme?

YES ↓

NO ←

Is it a 'contracted out' scheme?
See Chapter 7

YES ↓

You're already 'contracted out' of SERPS. Do nothing
See Chapter 7

23

Chart 4: Your pension choices if you work for yourself

YOUR OWN PENSION

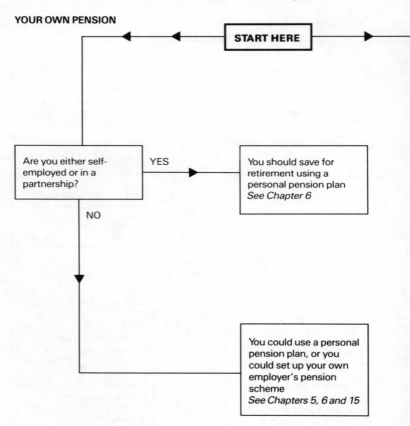

START HERE

Are you either self-employed or in a partnership?

YES

You should save for retirement using a personal pension plan
See Chapter 6

NO

You could use a personal pension plan, or you could set up your own employer's pension scheme
See Chapters 5, 6 and 15

YOUR STATE PENSION

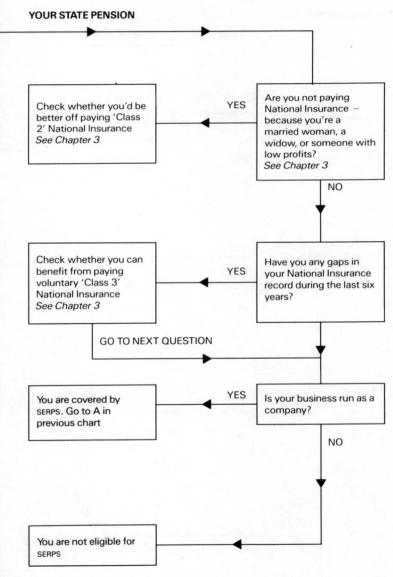

Check whether you'd be better off paying 'Class 2' National Insurance *See Chapter 3*

YES ◄──── Are you not paying National Insurance — because you're a married woman, a widow, or someone with low profits? *See Chapter 3*

NO

Check whether you can benefit from paying voluntary 'Class 3' National Insurance *See Chapter 3*

YES ◄──── Have you any gaps in your National Insurance record during the last six years?

GO TO NEXT QUESTION

You are covered by SERPS. Go to A in previous chart

YES ◄──── Is your business run as a company?

NO

You are not eligible for SERPS

Chart 5: Your pension choices if you're not working

YOUR OWN PENSION

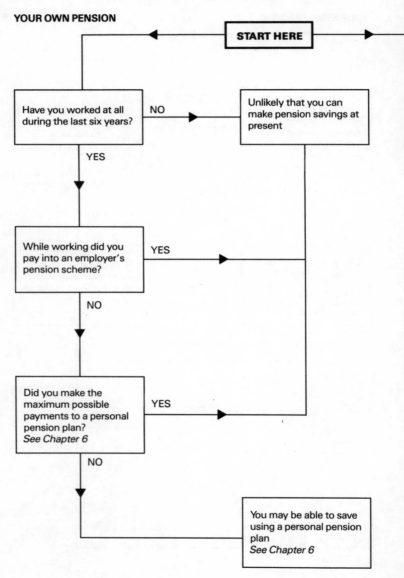

START HERE

Have you worked at all during the last six years?

NO → Unlikely that you can make pension savings at present

YES

While working did you pay into an employer's pension scheme?

YES →

NO

Did you make the maximum possible payments to a personal pension plan?
See Chapter 6

YES →

NO

You may be able to save using a personal pension plan
See Chapter 6

YOUR STATE PENSION

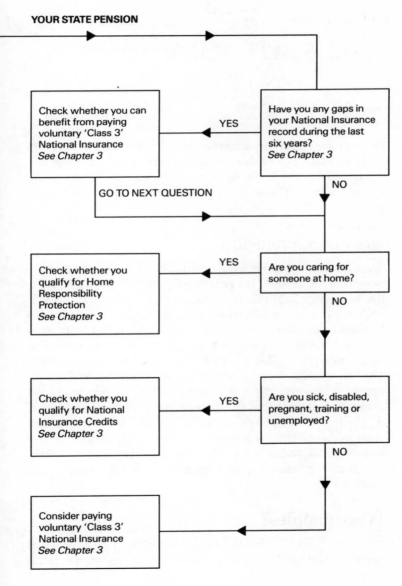

Check whether you can benefit from paying voluntary 'Class 3' National Insurance
See Chapter 3

Have you any gaps in your National Insurance record during the last six years?
See Chapter 3

YES

NO

GO TO NEXT QUESTION

Check whether you qualify for Home Responsibility Protection
See Chapter 3

Are you caring for someone at home?

YES

NO

Check whether you qualify for National Insurance Credits
See Chapter 3

Are you sick, disabled, pregnant, training or unemployed?

YES

NO

Consider paying voluntary 'Class 3' National Insurance
See Chapter 3

═══3═══

THE STATE BASIC PENSION

Some nine million pensioners receive a flat-rate basic pension from the state. For half of them, this is their only income; for many others, the basic pension provides the backbone of their retirement finances.

How much pension?

Basic pension is paid at a full rate of £46.90 a week for a single person in the 1990–91 **tax year** (a tax year runs from 6 April to the following 5 April). A married couple can qualify for a higher pension of £75.10 a week, which is based on the husband's pension entitlement. If both partners qualify for a full basic pension in their own right, they can each receive the single rate giving them 2 × £46.90 = £93.80 a week in total. The equivalent yearly amounts are shown in Table 5 opposite, together with the amounts for the previous four years. You can see that the pension has increased each year. At present, basic pensions are increased each April in line with price inflation (measured by the yearly change in the Retail Prices Index up to the previous September). State retirement pensioners also qualify for a £10 bonus each Christmas.

Who qualifies?

You qualify for state basic pension by building up a sufficient record of **National Insurance**. National Insurance is a tax paid

Table 5: Yearly rates of state basic pension [1]

	Single person	Married couple	Couple both with single pension
year	£	£	£
1990–91	2,438.80	3,905.20	4,877.60
1989–90	2,267.20	3,629.60	4,534.40
1988–89	2,139.80	3,426.80	4,279.60
1987–88	2,054.00	3,289.00	4,108.00
1986–87	2,012.40	3,221.40	4,024.80

[1] Excluding the Christmas bonus

by nearly everyone who works. If you don't work, you may be given National Insurance credits, or have your record protected in another way.

If you work for an employer

You pay **Class 1 National Insurance** provided your earnings are equal to, or more than, a **lower earnings limit**. The lower earnings limit is set by the government each year and is £46 a week, or its equivalent (for example, £200 a month or £2,392 a year) for the 1990–91 tax year. National Insurance on earnings up to the lower limit is charged at a rate of two per cent of those earnings, and counts towards the state basic pension.

If you earn less than the lower earnings limit, you don't pay National Insurance, and you're not building up state basic pension.

In the past, married women could choose to pay Class 1 National Insurance at a special reduced rate, whatever their earnings. This option was withdrawn from 6 April 1977, but if you'd already chosen to pay the lower contributions, you can carry on doing so (even if you've been widowed since then). However, married women's reduced rate contributions don't count towards state retirement pensions, so you might be better off choosing to pay at the full rate instead. Also, if your earnings are low, you may actually pay *more* at the reduced rate than you'd pay at the full rate – see p. 56.

If you work for yourself

If you're self-employed, you build up basic pension by paying **Class 2 National Insurance** at a flat rate – £4.55 a week in the 1990–91 tax year. You might also pay **Class 4 National Insurance**, but this doesn't count towards any state pensions or benefits.

If your profits are lower than a given limit – £2,600 for the 1990–91 tax year – you can choose not to pay Class 2 National Insurance. And, in the past, married women could choose not to make Class 2 payments, whatever their profits. This option was withdrawn from 6 April 1977, but if you'd already made this choice you can continue not to pay (even if you've subsequently been widowed). In both these cases, you're not building up state retirement pension so you might be better off paying Class 2 National Insurance after all.

Since 6 April 1975, if you're a director of your own company, you count as an employee and you build up basic pension by paying Class 1 National Insurance as described on p. 29.

If you're not working

In some situations you may be credited with National Insurance, even though you haven't paid it. This happens:

- if you're claiming certain state benefits, such as unemployment, maternity or sickness benefit
- if you're a man within five years of state pension age (see p. 33) and unemployed – you get the credits without having to 'sign on'
- for the years in which you have (or had) your sixteenth, seventeenth and eighteenth birthdays, if you were still at school and were born after 5 April 1957

- for the years in which you take part in an approved training course (but this doesn't include going to university), if you were born after 5 April 1957.

If you stay at home to care for your children, or a sick or elderly relative, you may qualify for **Home Responsibilities Protection**. Instead of getting credits, this protection reduces the length of National Insurance record that you need in order to qualify for a given level of basic pension. You can get Home Responsibilities Protection automatically if you're receiving child benefit. In other cases, you'll usually need to claim it (see p. 35).

If you don't qualify for credits or Home Responsibilities Protection, you may be able to pay voluntary **Class 3 National Insurance** in order to prevent there being a gap in your record. You can also use Class 3 payments to fill in earlier gaps in your record during the last six years. But you can't pay Class 3 National Insurance for any period when you had taken up the married women's option to pay National Insurance at the reduced rate or not at all.

Class 3 National Insurance is paid at a flat rate – £4.45 each in the 1990–91 tax year.

EXAMPLE

Megan left school aged 18 and went to university for three years. She is now 25 and earning a good salary working for a bank. She has National Insurance credits for the tax years in which she reached ages 16, 17 and 18, and she now makes Class 1 payments. But there is a gap in Megan's record for the three years she was at college. She could fill this by paying voluntary Class 3 National Insurance, but she shouldn't delay doing this much longer: after this year, she won't be able to pay contributions for the year in which she was 19 because it will be more than six years ago. Megan will still have time to make good the contributions for the years in which she reached ages 20 and 21.

Table 6: Do your contributions count towards basic pension?

Type of contribution	Description	Do they count?
Class 1 – full rate	paid by employees, including company directors [1], but not people earning less than the lower earnings limit	YES
Class 1 – reduced rate	paid by some married women and widows. (They can choose to switch to full rate)	NO
Class 2	paid by self-employed. Optional for people with profits below a given limit, and for some married women and widows	YES
Class 3	voluntary	YES
Class 4	paid by self-employed with profits above a given amount	NO

[1] Before 6 April 1975, company directors counted as self-employed

Paid too little National Insurance?

Whether or not you qualify for the full rate of basic pension depends on your record of National Insurance. If you have too few contributions, you may qualify for a reduced rate pension. If you've paid National Insurance for only a handful of years, you might not get any basic pension at all.

The appendix at the end of this chapter explains in detail how you qualify for the full rate pension, and how a reduced rate pension is calculated. You don't need to work this out for yourself: you can find out how much basic pension you qualify for by contacting the **Retirement Pensions Forecast and Advisory (RPFA) service** – see p. 36.

When is basic pension paid?

State retirement pensions are payable from the **state pension age** of 60 for women and 65 for men. Where a wife's pension is based on her husband's National Insurance record, it can't be paid before the husband reaches age 65. If the wife is then under age 60, the husband will receive the extra pension in respect of her; but, if the wife is aged 60 or over, the extra pension will be paid directly to her.

You can, of course, retire before you reach state pension age, but you'll have to make do without the state pension until you reach 60 or 65, as applicable.

You can put off starting to receive state pension for up to five years. Your eventual pension will be increased during that time by 7.5 per cent for each year you put it off. You can't defer taking state pension for longer than five years, as it becomes automatically payable at age 65 for women and age 70 for men. If you're under that age but you've already started to receive your pension, you can stop taking the pension and qualify for the increase.

Suppose you decide to put off taking your pension for five years – will it be a good deal? If you gave up a full basic pension for the 1990–91 tax year, you'd lose £46.90 a week or £2,439 for the year. Next year, you'd give up a bit more because the pension is increased each year to keep pace with inflation. But, if we look at the *buying power* of the pension you'd give up, next year you'd also lose £2,439 in terms of 1990–91 money. If you gave up the pension for five years, you'd lose $5 \times £2,439 = £12,194$ in terms of 1990–91 money. At the end of five years, you'd start to receive your pension, but at an increased rate. The increase would be 7.5 per cent for each of the five years, which comes to 37.5 per cent (the yearly increase is not **compounded**, meaning that the increase earned for one year is not itself increased in the following years). Still working in terms of 1990–91 money, the increase in your basic pension would be $37.5\% \times £46.90 = £17.59$ a week, or £914.55 a year. Dividing the £12,194 that you gave up by the £914.55 which you gain each year tells you how many years it will take until you've received as much pension as you gave up. The answer is $13\frac{1}{3}$ years. A man who starts to receive his deferred pension at age 70 would have to survive until age 83 to break even, but the life expectancy of the average 70-year-old man is only 10 years (see p. 9). A woman starting to receive her deferred pension at age 65 would have to survive until age 78 to break even. She's likely to do this, because the life expectancy of the average 65-year-old woman is 17 years (see p. 9). Deferring your pension for five years will generally appear worthwhile for a woman, but not for a man.

EXAMPLE

Iain will be 65 in three months' time. He runs his own business and doesn't intend to stop working yet, so he's thinking that he might put off taking his state pension for a while. He'd be giving up £2,439 a year, in terms of today's money. In return, once his pension started to be paid, it would be well over a third higher than the normal rate of pension – just under £65 a week instead of £46.90, in today's money. But that's not as tempting as it might seem: he'd need to be aged 83 before he'd received more pension than he gave up. Iain would need to live significantly longer than is average for a man of his age in order to profit from deferring his pension. He decides not to defer his pension. Instead, he starts to receive it at age 65, and uses it to bring forward spending on maintaining and improving his house.

You don't have to stop working in order to qualify for state pension. Basic pension used to be reduced if it was paid to you but you earned above a certain amount during the first five years after reaching state pension age. From 1 October 1989, this is no longer the case: the amount of your state pension is now unaffected by any earnings you have after reaching pension age.

More information

Your main source of information about state pensions is the **Department of Social Security (DSS).** You can find out where your nearest DSS office is by looking in the telephone book under 'Social Security, Department of'. In older telephone books, you may have to look under 'Health and Social Security, Department of'.

DSS offices can either answer your questions or pass on your queries to the relevant section. If you have a general query, rather than one specific to your particular case, you can get information by telephoning Freeline Social Security: (0800) 666555.

Table 7: State basic pension: useful DSS leaflets

Leaflet number	Leaflet name
NP27	Looking after someone at home? How to protect your pension
NP46	A guide to state retirement pensions
SA29	Your social security and pension rights in the European Community
NI1	National Insurance for married women
NI27A	National Insurance for people with small earnings from self-employment
NI35	National Insurance for company directors
NI40	National Insurance for employees
NI41	National Insurance guide for the self-employed
NI42	National Insurance voluntary contributions
NI48	National Insurance – late and unpaid contributions
NI51	National Insurance for widows
NI125	Training for further employment and your National Insurance record

The DSS will handle any claims that you make, supply forms that you need, and are a source of information leaflets. You can also order DSS leaflets from ISCO5 (DSS) (address on p. 214). Table 7 on the previous page lists DSS leaflets that you may find particularly useful when you're considering your state basic pension entitlement.

The DSS runs a **Retirement Pension Forecast and Advice (RPFA)** service which will provide you with details of the state pension you've built up so far, and your expected pension at retirement if your circumstances continue unchanged. The service will also indicate any steps that you could take to increase your entitlement – for example, paying Class 3 National Insurance to fill in gaps, or switching from the married women's reduced rate to full rate Class 1 payments. It gives you details and forecasts of your basic pension and also any state earnings-related and graduated pensions for which you qualify. You're allowed to have up to one forecast a year. To use the service, get *Form BR19* from any DSS office, complete it and send it to the RPFA Unit (address on p. 215). Expect to wait several weeks for a reply.

APPENDIX TO CHAPTER 3

How you qualify for basic pension

Do you have enough National Insurance each year?

How much pension you get depends on how many **qualifying years** of National Insurance you have. A 'qualifying year' is generally a tax year in which you've paid the required National Insurance. It's possible to pay some National Insurance during a year but not enough for the year to count towards your pension. Table 8 below shows how many contributions you need for a year to count towards your basic

Table 8: How much National Insurance makes a qualifying year [1]

Type of payment	How many payments are needed for a tax year to count towards basic pension
Class 1	payments on earnings equal to, or more than, 52 times the weekly lower earnings limit
Class 2	52 payments
Class 3	52 payments

[1] The information in this table applies from 6 April 1975, except for Class 1 National Insurance where it applies from 6 April 1978. Up to 5 April 1975, both employees (except those on low earnings) and the self-employed paid National Insurance at a single rate. All these payments are added together and divided into 'lots' of 50. Each 'lot' counts as a year's worth of National Insurance, as does any remaining part-'lot'. From 6 April 1975 to 5 April 1978, Class 1 payments on earnings of at least 50 (not 52) times the lower earnings limit were enough for the year to count towards the basic pension

pension. A qualifying year doesn't have to be made up of payments all of the same type; you could, for example, have a mixture of Class 1 and Class 3 National Insurance, or Class 2 and Class 1. A Class 1 payment on earnings equal to the weekly lower earnings limit is equivalent to one Class 2 or Class 3 payment.

Do you have enough qualifying years in your working life?

If at least 90 per cent of the years in your **working life** are

Table 9: How much state basic pension you'll get [1]

Number of years which are qualifying and count towards your state basic pension	Percentage of the full basic pension for which you qualify	
	if you are a woman	if you are a man
9 or less	0	0
10	26	0
11	29	25
12	31	28
13	34	30
14	36	32
15	39	35
16	42	37
17	44	39
18	47	41
19	49	44
20	52	46
21	54	48
22	57	50
23	59	53
24	62	55
25	65	57
26	67	60

[1] If your working life is shorter than 44 years (women) or 49 years (men), this table does not apply. See instead p. 40

qualifying years, you should get the full basic pension. If you have fewer qualifying years, you'll normally get a reduced rate of pension. But, if fewer than a quarter of the years in your working life are qualifying ones, you might not be entitled to any basic pension at all.

'Working life' is an official definition. For most people, it means the tax years from the one in which you reach age 16 up to the last complete tax year before you reach state pension age. Most women have a working life of 44 years and most men have a working life of 49 years. Your working life

Number of years which are qualifying and count towards your state basic pension	Percentage of the full basic pension for which you qualify	
	if you are a woman	if you are a man
27	70	62
28	72	64
29	75	66
30	77	69
31	80	71
32	83	73
33	85	75
34	88	78
35	90	80
36	93	82
37	95	85
38	98	87
39	100	89
40	100	91
41	100	94
42	100	96
43	100	98
44 or more	100	100

may be shorter than this, if you were born before 5 July 1932. In this case, you should read the section *If you are older* below.

Table 9 on pp. 38 and 39 shows what percentage of the full basic pension you'll get, depending on the number of qualifying years you've built up and assuming that your working life is 44 years if you're a woman, or 49 years if you're a man.

EXAMPLE

Peggy is 55. Her working life runs from the tax year in which she reached age 16 to the last tax year before she'll reach age 60 – 44 years in total. So far, Peggy has 28 qualifying years which she built up before she married and since going back to work when her children started secondary school. This would entitle her to a basic pension of just under three-quarters (72 per cent) of the full rate – in other words, £33.77 a week at the 1990–91 pension rate. If she carries on making contributions until pension age, she'll build up 32 qualifying years which will entitle her to a pension of 83 per cent of the full rate – £38.93 at the 1990–91 pension rate.

If you are older

The present system of basic pensions started on 5 July 1948. If you were already 16 on that date, the system could work unfairly if your working life were deemed to have started at that age. Therefore, special rules exist which can protect your pension position, if you were born before 5 July 1932. They work by reducing the length of your working life and, thus, the number of years of contributions which you need in order to qualify for a given level of basic pension. Chart 6 opposite shows how the rules affect you.

Chart 7 on pp. 42 and 43 shows the percentage of the full rate of basic pension that you're entitled to, given the length of your working life and the number of qualifying contribution years that you have.

Chart 6: How long is your working life?

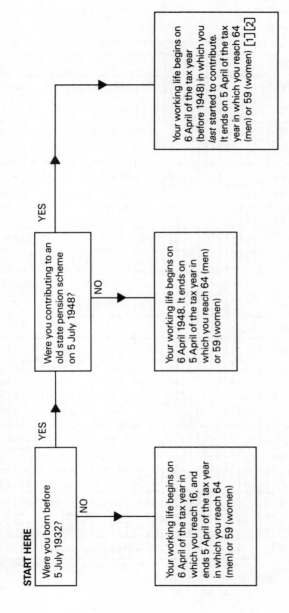

START HERE

Were you born before 5 July 1932?

NO

Your working life begins on 6 April of the tax year in which you reach 16, and ends 5 April of the tax year in which you reach 64 (men) or 59 (women)

YES

Were you contributing to an old state pension scheme on 5 July 1948?

NO

Your working life begins on 6 April 1948. It ends on 5 April of the tax year in which you reach 64 (men) or 59 (women)

YES

Your working life begins on 6 April of the tax year (before 1948) in which you *last* started to contribute. It ends on 5 April of the tax year in which you reach 64 (men) or 59 (women) [1] [2]

[1] If your working life began before 5 July 1948, you are credited with the contributions for each week from the start of your working life up to 5 July 1948

[2] For people who had been contributing since 6 April 1936, working life began on 6 April 1936

41

Chart 7: How much basic pension you're entitled to

Number of years in working life

	27	28	29	30	31	32	33	34	35	36	37	38	39	40	41	42	43	44	45	46	47	48	49
1																							
2																							
3																							
4																							
5																							
6	25																						
7	30	28	27	26	26	25	25																
8	34	32	31	30	30	29	28	27	26	25	25												
9	38	36	35	34	34	33	32	30	30	29	28	27	26	25	25	25							
10	42	40	39	38	38	36	35	34	33	32	31	30	29	28	28	28	27	26	25	25			
11	46	44	43	41	41	40	38	37	36	35	34	33	32	31	31	30	29	29	28	27	27	26	25
12	50	48	47	45	45	43	42	40	39	38	37	36	35	34	34	33	32	31	30	30	29	28	28
13	55	52	50	49	49	47	45	44	42	41	40	39	38	37	37	36	35	34	33	32	31	31	30
14	59	56	54	52	52	50	49	47	46	44	43	42	41	39	39	38	37	36	35	35	34	33	32
15	63	60	58	56	56	54	52	50	49	47	46	45	43	42	42	41	40	39	38	37	36	35	35
16	67	64	62	60	60	58	56	54	52	50	49	48	46	45	45	44	43	42	40	40	39	38	37
17	71	68	66	63	63	61	59	57	55	54	52	50	49	48	48	46	45	44	43	42	41	40	39
18	75	72	70	67	67	65	63	60	59	57	55	53	52	50	50	49	48	47	45	44	43	42	41
19	80	76	74	71	71	68	66	64	62	60	58	56	55	53	53	52	50	49	48	47	46	45	44
20	84	80	77	75	75	72	69	67	65	63	61	59	58	56	56	55	53	52	50	49	48	47	46
21	88	84	81	78	78	75	73	70	68	66	64	62	60	59	59	57	56	54	53	52	50	49	48
22	92	88	85	82	82	79	76	74	71	69	67	65	63	62	62	60	58	57	55	54	53	52	50
23	96	92	89	86	86	83	80	77	75	72	70	68	66	64	64	63	61	59	58	57	55	54	53

Basic pension as a percentage of the full rate. Rows = number of years of contributions which count towards basic pension; columns = years of working life.

Contributions \ Working life	49	48	47	46	45	44	43	42	41	40	39	38	37	36	35	34	33	32	31	30	29	28	27	26	25	24
24	55	56	58	59	59	60	62	64	65	67	69	71	73	75	75	78	80	83	86	89	93	96	100	100	100	100
25	57	59	60	61	61	63	65	66	68	70	72	74	76	79	79	81	84	87	90	93	97	100	100	100	100	
26	60	61	62	64	64	65	67	69	71	73	75	77	79	82	82	84	87	90	93	97	100	100	100	100		
27	62	63	65	66	66	68	70	72	73	75	78	80	82	85	85	88	90	94	97	100	100	100	100			
28	64	66	67	69	69	70	72	74	76	78	80	83	85	88	88	91	94	97	100	100	100	100				
29	66	68	69	71	71	73	75	77	79	81	83	86	88	91	91	94	97	100	100	100	100					
30	69	70	72	74	74	75	77	79	82	84	86	89	91	94	94	97	100	100	100	100						
31	71	73	74	76	76	78	80	82	84	87	89	92	94	97	97	100	100	100	100							
32	73	75	77	78	78	80	83	85	87	89	92	95	97	100	100	100	100	100								
33	75	77	79	81	81	83	85	87	90	92	95	98	100	100	100	100	100									
34	78	80	81	83	83	85	88	90	92	95	98	100	100	100	100	100										
35	80	82	84	86	86	88	90	93	95	98	100	100	100	100	100											
36	82	84	86	88	88	90	93	95	98	100	100	100	100	100												
37	85	86	89	91	91	93	95	98	100	100	100	100	100													
38	87	89	91	93	93	95	98	100	100	100	100	100														
39	89	91	93	96	96	98	100	100	100	100	100															
40	91	93	96	98	98	100	100	100	100	100																
41	94	96	98	100	100	100	100	100	100																	
42	96	98	100	100	100	100	100	100																		
43	98	100	100	100	100	100	100																			
44	100	100	100	100	100	100																				
45	100	100	100	100	100																					
46	100	100	100	100																						
47	100	100	100																							
48	100	100																								
49	100																									

Number of years of contributions which count towards basic pension

EXAMPLE

Leonard was born on 7 September 1927. He wasn't working on 5 July 1948, so his working life started on 6 April 1948 and runs until 5 April 1992 – a total of 44 years, instead of the usual 49 years for a man. Leonard needs only 39 years of contributions in order to qualify for a full basic pension instead of the usual 43 years.

Unfortunately, a few people – mainly women who married and stopped work before July 1948 – lose out under the rules because National Insurance they paid before they were married falls outside the definition of their working life and no longer counts towards their pension.

=4=

STATE EARNINGS RELATED PENSIONS

The State Earnings Related Pension Scheme (SERPS)

How much pension?

State Earnings Related Pension Scheme (SERPS) pensions are additional state pensions which many people build up through paying Class 1 National Insurance. As the name suggests, SERPS pensions are linked to your earnings and so the amount received varies from person to person.

Your SERPS pension is worked out using a complicated formula. Thankfully, you don't need to be able to work it out for yourself, as the DSS will provide you with a statement of your SERPS entitlement (see p. 36). For those who'd like to know more about how SERPS pensions are calculated, the appendix to this chapter gives details. Here, we give just a broad outline.

SERPS pensions are based on your earnings. Not all earnings are taken into account – only those over the lower earnings limit and up to an **upper earnings limit**. The upper earnings limit is set by the government each year and is £350 a week for the 1990–91 tax year. The pension is based on the average of these earnings over your whole working life, or your working life since 6 April 1978 if you reached age 16 before that date (but see the appendix if you'll reach state pension age before 6 April 1999). The amount of pension you qualify for is increased in line with earnings inflation up to the time you reach state pension age, and increases in line with price inflation once it's being paid.

If your earnings are equal to or above the upper earnings limit throughout your whole working life, you'll qualify for the maximum SERPS pension possible. Table 10 below gives a rough guide to the maximum SERPS pension you might get in today's money, and based on the 1990–91 earnings limits. The amount varies according to when you reach state pension age largely because of changes that have been made to the SERPS system. If your earnings are at any time lower than the upper earnings limit, or you didn't belong to SERPS for part of your working life, your SERPS pension will be smaller than the amounts shown in the table. SERPS pensions can be any amount from nothing up to the maximum shown in the table.

Table 10: Guide to the maximum SERPS pension you could have

If you reach state pension age in the tax year:	The maximum SERPS pension in 1990–91 £££ [1]	
	£ a week	£ a year
1990–91	46	2,390
1995–96	65	3,380
2000–01	75	3,900
2005–06	70	3,640
2010–11	66	3,430
2020–21	64	3,330
2030–31 men	63	3,280
women	62	3,220
2040–41 and after	61	3,170

[1] The table assumes that you're a member of SERPS for as many years as possible. It also makes a simplifying assumption that earnings rise at the same rate as prices (this results in a tendency to underestimate the amount of pension)

EXAMPLE

Jonathan started work in 1966 and joined SERPS when it started in 1978. He'll reach the state pension age of 65 in 2010. If he was in SERPS for the whole of that time, and earned at least as much as the upper earnings limit each year, he'd qualify for a SERPS pension of £3,430 a year, in today's money. In fact, he's earned consistently less than the upper earnings limit and looks likely to have an eventual SERPS pension of only half that amount.

Who qualifies?

You can be in SERPS only if you count as an employee; you're not in SERPS during any periods when you're self-employed. In some circumstances, you can belong to SERPS, but not build up SERPS pension; during these periods, your earnings for SERPS purposes count as zero. Since, for anyone retiring from 6 April 1999 onwards, SERPS pension is based on earnings in *all* the years in your working life (or since 6 April 1978), periods of zero earnings will reduce your eventual pension. You'll be deemed to have zero earnings for SERPS purposes in the following situations:

- if you're low-paid. If you earn less than the lower earnings limit (£46 per week in the 1990–91 tax year – see p. 29). You pay no National Insurance and build up neither basic nor SERPS pension
- if you're a married woman paying National Insurance at the married woman's reduced rate (see p. 29)
- if you're paying voluntary Class 3 National Insurance (see p. 31). These count only towards the state basic pension, not SERPS
- if you're unemployed. Though you get National Insurance credits (see p. 30), these count only towards the basic pension, not SERPS.

If you stay at home to care for children, or for a sick or elderly relative, you may qualify for Home Responsibilities Protection (see p. 31). For anyone reaching state pension age on or after 6 April 1999, though you won't build up any SERPS pension while you qualify for Home Responsibilities Protection, these periods are not counted in your SERPS record at all and can't reduce the pension that you eventually get. Your SERPS record is protected in a similar way, if you're getting National Insurance credits because you're incapable of work – because you are ill or disabled, for example. But, in either of these cases, the part of your working life which counts towards SERPS can't be reduced to fewer than 20 years. These measures don't apply to people reaching state pension age before 6 April 1999.

When is SERPS paid?

SERPS pension can be paid once you reach the state pension age – 60 for women and 65 for men. If you put off starting to receive your state basic pension (see p. 33), you'll also have to put off taking your SERPS pension. The deferred SERPS pension will be increased by 7.5 per cent for each year, in the same way as the deferred basic pension. The longest time you can put off starting to take your pension is five years – SERPS pensions, as well as basic pensions, are automatically paid once you reach age 65 if you're a woman, or 70 if you're a man.

Graduated pensions

There was an old state earnings-related pension scheme, which ran from 6 April 1961 to 5 April 1975 and provided **graduated pensions**. If you belonged to the scheme, the National Insurance you paid was related to your earnings. The total that you paid is divided into units: if you're a woman, every £9 you paid counts as one unit; if you're a man, every £7.50 that you paid counts as a unit.

48

How much pension you get depends on how many units you have. In the 1990–91 tax year, each unit is worth 6.14 pence a week. This means that the biggest graduated pension a man could have is £5.29 a week. The biggest graduated pension a woman could have is £4.42. Though graduated pensions are now increased each year in line with price inflation, they will never be large pensions. The scheme wasn't designed to cope with the very high rates of inflation that Britain experienced during the 1970s; the buying power of graduated pensions was badly eroded during that time and there's no mechanism for allowing it to catch up.

As with the SERPS scheme, you may have been contracted-out of the graduated pension scheme, which meant that your employer took over the responsibility of paying you an equivalent amount of pension at retirement – called the **Equivalent Pension Benefit** or EPB.

More information

Your main source of help and information about SERPS and graduated pensions is the Department of Social Security (DSS) – see p. 35. The DSS produces the following leaflets which may be helpful, if you're looking at your earnings-related pension entitlements:

Table 11: State Earnings Related Pension: useful DSS leaflets

NP27	Looking after someone at home? How to protect your pension
NP46	A guide to state retirement pensions
NI40	National Insurance for employees

You can get a statement of your current SERPS (and other state pensions) entitlement and a forecast of what it could be by retirement by contacting the Retirement Pension Forecast and Advice (RPFA) service – see p. 36. The service will provide details of any graduated pension you qualify for as well. Complete *Form BR19* (from DSS offices) and return it to the RPFA Unit (address on p. 215).

APPENDIX TO CHAPTER 4

How to work out your SERPS pension

You don't need to work out your SERPS pension for yourself – the DSS will do that for you. To do the calculations yourself requires some numerical skills and a certain amount of foraging for figures. You are not recommended to try to calculate the figures for yourself. If, however, you wish to know more about the way in which SERPS pensions are calculated, here is an outline.

Step 1 For each year since April 1978, earnings on which you've paid Class 1 contributions at the full rate are taken. This will be all your earnings if you earn less than the upper earnings limit, or your earnings up to that limit if you earn more. (Any earnings above the upper earnings limit are ignored.) The upper earnings limits for each year are shown in Table 12 overleaf.

Step 2 Each year's earnings are increased in line with changes in national average earnings – these are called your **revalued earnings**.

Step 3 The lower earnings limit for the year in which you retire is subtracted from each year's revalued earnings. What's left is called your **surplus earnings**.

Step 4 Your SERPS pension is a fraction of your surplus

Table 12: Upper earnings limits since April 1978

Tax year	Weekly limit	Monthly equivalent	Yearly equivalent
1978–79	£120	£520.00	£ 6,240.00
1979–80	£135	£585.00	£ 7,020.00
1980–81	£165	£715.00	£ 8,580.00
1981–82	£200	£866.67	£10,400.04
1982–83	£220	£953.33	£11,439.96
1983–84	£235	£1,018.33	£12,219.96
1984–85	£250	£1,083.33	£12,999.96
1985–86	£265	£1,148.33	£13,779.96
1986–87	£285	£1,235.00	£14,820.00
1987–88	£295	£1,279.00	£15,340.00
1988–89	£305	£1,322.00	£15,860.00
1989–90	£325	£1,408.33	£16,900.00
1990–91	£350	£1,516.67	£18,200.00

earnings. The fraction, or fractions, used depends on when you retire:

- if you retire on or before 5 April 1999, you get one-eightieth of each year's surplus earnings (up to a maximum of 20 years). This means that the most SERPS pension you can have is a quarter ($20 \times \frac{1}{80}$) of your average surplus earnings
- if you retire after 5 April 1999, the fraction is gradually reduced until, eventually, the biggest SERPS pension will be one-fifth of your average surplus earnings.

Chart 8 on pp. 54 and 55 summarises the four steps.

EXAMPLE

Alfred retired in late 1988, aged 65. He'd been in SERPS since 6 April 1983. His SERPS pension was worked out as follows:

Step 1   His earnings for each year are shown in column 1 of the table below. They were all below the upper earnings limits, and so they all counted towards SERPS.

Step 2   Alfred's earnings were revalued in line with average earnings up to the last complete tax year (1987–88) before he reached the state pension age of 65. This gave revalued earnings as shown in column 2 of the table.

Step 3   The lower earnings limit, which was a yearly amount of £2,028 when Alfred retired, is deducted from each revalued earnings figure to leave the surplus earnings shown in column 3 of the table.

Step 4   Adding together one-eightieth of the surplus earnings for each year gave £159 + £161 + £161 + £172 + £77 = £730. In other words, Alfred was entitled to a SERPS pension of £14.04 a week. Since retiring, this has been increased each year in line with changes in the Retail Prices Index.

Year	Alfred's earnings	Revalued earnings	Surplus earnings
	1	*2*	*3*
1983–84	£10,070	£14,742	£12,714
1984–85	£11,000	£14,916	£12,888
1985–86	£11,700	£14,882	£12,854
1986–87	£13,500	£15,768	£13,740
1987–88	£ 8,200	£ 8,200	£ 6,172

Chart 8: How your SERPS pension is worked out

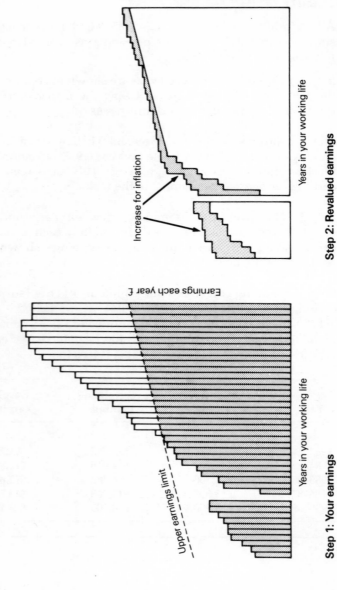

Step 1: Your earnings

Earnings each year £

Upper earnings limit

Years in your working life

Step 2: Revalued earnings

Revalued earnings for each year £

Increase for inflation

Years in your working life

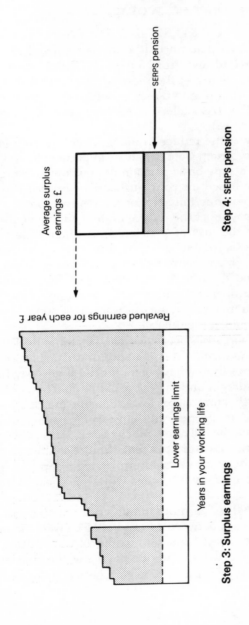

Average surplus earnings £

SERPS pension

Step 4: SERPS pension

Revalued earnings for each year £

Lower earnings limit

Years in your working life

Step 3: Surplus earnings

A note for married women

Married women and widows used to be able to choose to pay Class 1 National Insurance at a special reduced rate. This option was withdrawn from 6 April 1977, but women who were already paying at the reduced rate at that date have been able to continue to do so, provided they meet certain conditions. (See DSS leaflet *NI1 National Insurance for married women* for details.)

If you pay at the reduced rate, you can't qualify in your own right for certain state benefits – in particular, you're not building up a state basic pension of your own (though you may get one based on your husband's National Insurance record) and you don't qualify for a SERPS pension.

If you're paying at the reduced rate, you'll have to weigh up whether the loss of pension (and other state benefit) entitlements is outweighed by the saving in National Insurance payments – this will vary depending on your (and your husband's) particular circumstances. But, if you're on fairly low earnings, you might not be saving any money at all – in fact, you may be paying out *more* in National Insurance than you would at the full rate.

This situation arises because, since 1 October 1989, full-rate National Insurance on the first slice of earnings – up to the lower earnings limit – has been reduced if you pay full-rate National Insurance and earn at, or above, that limit. The 2 per cent rate on that first slice is lower than the married women's reduced rate of 3.85 per cent. On earnings above the lower earnings limit, the full rate is much higher (9 per cent if you're contracted into SERPS or 7 per cent if you're contracted out), so for married women on medium or high earnings paying at the reduced rate will always work out cheaper than the full rate.

At the 1990–91 earnings limits and National Insurance rates, if you earn between £46 and £62.51 a week (inclusive), you would pay less National Insurance by switching to the full rate, if you would then be paying at the contracted-in National Insurance rate. If you earn between £46 and £73.01

(inclusive), you would pay less by switching to the full rate, if you would then be paying at the contracted-out rate.

Once you switch to the full rate of National insurance, you can't ever switch back to the reduced rate. The amount of earnings up to which the reduced rate works out as more expensive will rise each year as the lower earnings limit is increased. But, if you expect your earnings to rise faster than that, paying at the reduced rate might save you money at some time in the future even though it doesn't now. If you think your earnings will rise appreciably, you're back in the position of weighing up the pros and cons of your position. But, if you expect to remain a relatively low earner, you should consider switching to full rate National Insurance. Your local DSS office can advise you, and DSS leaflet NI1 contains details of how to make the switch.

=5=

EMPLOYERS' PENSION SCHEMES

Many employers set up and run schemes which are designed to provide retirement pensions for their employees, and often other benefits as well, such as life insurance and pensions for widows and children. Employers' schemes are attractive ways of saving for retirement because your employer pays in money on your behalf, and most schemes qualify for the following tax reliefs:

- you and your employer both get tax relief on contributions to the scheme
- the invested contributions build up tax-free
- part of the proceeds can usually be taken as a tax-free lump sum at retirement.

Who qualifies?

A scheme may be open to all employees, or restricted to employees in a particular group – for example, there might be one scheme for works staff and another for management.

If your employer runs a scheme for which you are eligible, you don't have to join it; and, if you're already a member, you can leave the scheme. But there may be restrictions on joining or rejoining the scheme later on, for example, the scheme might not accept employees over a certain age, or it might not be open to employees who were previously members but had chosen to leave.

Not all employers have a pension scheme. If you're not

covered by an employer's scheme, you should look into making your own pension arrangements (see Chapter 6).

How much pension?

How much pension you build up depends in part on the type of scheme that you belong to. There are two main types of employers' pension schemes: **final pay schemes** (also called **final salary schemes**, and they are the most common type of **defined benefit scheme**) and **money purchase schemes** (also called **defined contribution schemes**).

Final pay schemes

The majority of people in an employer's pension scheme belong to this type of scheme. The pension you get depends on your pay at, or near, retirement and the number of years that you've been in the scheme. For example, you might get one-eightieth or one-sixtieth of your pre-retirement pay for each year in the scheme. The major advantages of final pay schemes are that your pension entitlement generally keeps pace with changes in your earnings while you are working, and you have a good idea of how much pension you'll eventually get in terms of your earnings just before retirement. This gives you a guide to the standard of living you can afford in retirement and helps you to work out whether you're saving enough.

But final pay schemes can be unattractive, if you expect to change jobs before retirement (see Chapter 8), though there have been major improvements in this area.

'Final pay' will be defined in the scheme's rules. It can have a variety of meanings – for example, pay at a specified date, your average pay over the last three years, the best three years' pay out of the last ten, and so on.

'Pay' may mean just your basic salary, or it might be defined to include overtime pay, bonuses, commission, and so on. Some schemes adjust the pension they'll pay you to take account of the basic pension you can get from the state. In this case, 'pay' may be your earnings less a slice equal to the amount of the state basic pension, or some multiple of it.

EXAMPLE

The bank that Megan works for runs a final pay pension scheme. Megan has been a member for only four years so far, but if she makes a career with the bank until the normal retirement age of 60, she'll have 39 years' membership. The scheme pays a pension of one-sixtieth of final pay for each year, so she could qualify for a pension equal to nearly two-thirds of her pre-retirement earnings ($39 \times \frac{1}{60} \times$ final pay).

Money purchase schemes

With these, your pension depends on the amount you and your employer contribute, how well the invested contributions grow, and how much pension the investment will 'buy' when you reach retirement. Unlike final pay schemes, there's no automatic link between your pay and your pension, and you can't tell in advance how much pension you'll get in the end. This makes retirement planning a bit more difficult. But, with this type of scheme, your expected pension isn't usually affected by job changes (see Chapter 8).

EXAMPLE

Angela is 41 and earns £10,000 a year working for a small travel agency. They run a money purchase scheme for their staff. Angela pays in five per cent of her pay, and the company pays in an amount equal to another eight per cent of her pay. The bulk of these contributions is invested to build up a cash fund which will be used at retirement to provide

Angela with a pension. At this stage, it's impossible to say how much pension she'll get, but, if she stayed with the company until retirement, and if the invested contributions grew by, say, four per cent a year more than price inflation, her cash fund might provide a pension at retirement of £4,700 a year in today's prices – or somewhat less, if the pension were guaranteed to increase throughout her retirement.

Hybrid schemes

Some employers run pension schemes which combine final pay and money purchase elements. For example, the scheme may usually pay out a money purchase pension but also guarantee that the amount won't be less than a pension worked out according to a final pay formula. Another scheme might usually pay out final pay pensions but guarantee that you'll get the full value of a notional cash fund worked out according to money purchase principles. Hybrid schemes attempt to combine the best of both worlds by providing pensions which tend to keep pace with earnings and which are also largely unaffected by job moves.

EXAMPLE

Jonathan is a magazine journalist. His employer runs a 'hybrid' pension scheme. Jonathan and his employer each put an amount equal to five per cent of his salary into a pension fund which will provide a cash sum at retirement to 'buy' Jonathan's pension – in other words, this is a money purchase arrangement. But, Jonathan's employer also pays an amount – currently equal to three per cent of the salary bill – into another fund which provides a sort of safety net. This enables the employer to guarantee that Jonathan's pension will not be less than one-hundredth of his final pay for each year of membership of the scheme.

Other types of scheme

There are a number of other less common types of pension scheme, which generally provide poorer pensions than final pay or money purchase schemes. These include:

- **average pay schemes**   These work like final pay schemes, except that your pension is based on pay throughout your working life, rather than pay near retirement. In a good scheme, pay from the earlier years will have been adjusted to take account of inflation before your pension is worked out. (An average pay scheme which revalues pay from the earlier years can be even better than a final pay scheme for someone whose earnings peak in the middle of their working life)
- **salary grade schemes**   You 'earn' a set amount of pension for each year that your pay is within a specified band of earnings. The higher the earnings band, the greater the amount of pension
- **flat rate schemes**   You get a fixed amount of pension for each year that you're in the scheme.

Tax-free cash at retirement

Some schemes – especially those covering people who work for the public sector, for example, civil servants, teachers, local government staff, and so on – automatically provide a cash lump sum at retirement as well as a pension. With other schemes, you can choose to swap part of your pension for a lump sum.

Obviously, swapping pension for lump sum means that your remaining pension will be smaller. How much smaller depends on your particular scheme. Commonly, a woman retiring at age 60 might give up £1 a year of pension for each £11 of lump sum. A man retiring at 65 might give up £1 of pension for £9 of lump sum.

Usually, taking the lump sum is a good idea because it's completely tax-free, whereas the pension is taxed as income in the normal way. If taking a lump sum would reduce your pension to less than you need, it's often still worth taking it, but then using it to invest in a **purchased life annuity** from an insurance company. A purchased life annuity provides you with an income for life in exchange for a lump sum. Once you've made the investment you can't get your money back as a lump sum, but part of each annuity payment is treated as the return of your original investment. This part is tax-free; only the remaining income is taxable. This means you pay less tax on the total annuity 'income' than you'd pay on the same amount in pension from your pension scheme.

EXAMPLE

Iain is about to retire and is entitled to a pension of £9,200 a year from his employer's pension scheme. But Iain can take up to £20,700 as a tax-free lump sum. If he does this, his pension will be reduced to £6,900 a year.

Iain also qualifies for a state basic pension of £2,439 a year, so if he didn't take the lump sum, he'd have a total before-tax income of £11,639 a year. After tax, he'd have £9,729.

If, instead, Iain took the full lump sum and suppose he could invest in a purchased life annuity which would provide him with an income of £2,300 a year, his total before-tax income would still be £11,639 (£6,900 + £2,439 + £2,300) a year but, after tax, it would be £10,104. In practice, Iain's full lump sum could normally buy an annuity providing even more than £2,300 a year. Iain decides to take the lump sum.

In some situations, you should be wary of giving up your pension for a lump sum. For example, some employers' schemes (mainly in the public sector) provide pensions which are guaranteed to increase in line with inflation. Others don't guarantee to do this, but have a track record of paying good increases to their pensioners. Guaranteed increases may be taken into account in working out the lump sum, but non-guaranteed increases are not. Think twice before giving up these pensions as your lump sum probably wouldn't be enough to fully replace them.

In most schemes, taking a lump sum reduces your own pension, but not any pensions for widows or children (see Chapter 9). If your health is poor, it may be a good idea to take the biggest lump sum that you can at the time you retire.

Inland Revenue limits

Employers' pension schemes benefit from significant tax advantages, and so the Inland Revenue puts some limits on the amount of pension, and other benefits, that such schemes can provide. The main limits are set out in Table 13 opposite. They are set in relation to a definition of final pay which is specified in the tax legislation. 'Final pay' is usually:

- your earnings in any one year out of the last five years before retirement
- the yearly average of your earnings during a three-year period ending any time within the last ten years before retirement. This is the more commonly-used limit, and the one which usually must be used if you're a director of your own company.

Bear in mind that these are the Inland Revenue's definitions – your employer's scheme may choose to use definitions which are less generous.

If your employer's scheme is unusually generous, or if the Inland Revenue definition of final pay results in your pension benefits being limited to less than the available investment fund could 'buy', the earnings used to calculate final pay can be increased, up to retirement, in line with the relevant change in the Retail Prices Index. This process is called **dynamisation** and it effectively raises the Inland Revenue limits on all your benefits.

Normally, the maximum pension and other benefits build up over a period of 40 years: pension builds up at a rate of one-sixtieth of final pay for each year you're with the

Table 13: Main tax limits on your pension from an employer's scheme

Description of the scheme	Limit on your pension at retirement	Limit on your lump sum
Scheme you joined before 1 June 1989 and set up before 14 March 1989	$\frac{2}{3}$ of your final pay [1]	1½ times your final pay [2]
Scheme you joined on or after 1 June 1989 or set up on or after 14 March 1989	$\frac{2}{3}$ of your final pay [1] up to a maximum pension of £43,200 a year [3]	1½ times your final pay up to a maximum of lump sum of £97,200 [3]
All schemes	*After retirement* Pensions being paid can be increased as long as they don't exceed the maximum possible pension increased in line with changes in the Retail Prices Index	

[1] This limit is reduced in line with any tax-free lump that you receive
[2] For schemes that you joined between 17 March 1987 and 13 March 1989 inclusive, an overall cash limit of £150,000 also applies
[3] This is the limit proposed for the 1990–91 tax year. The limit will be increased each year in line with changes in the Retail Prices Index

employer; the lump sum builds up at a rate of three-eightieths of final pay for each year.

Alternatively, the rules allow a faster rate of build-up which can be useful, especially for executives and high-fliers who (or whose employers) want to boost their pension late on in their working lives. Different tax rules apply according to when a scheme was set up, or when you joined a scheme. If you joined your scheme before 17 March 1987, you need to have belonged to the scheme, by the time you reach retirement, for at least ten years in order to qualify for the two-thirds maximum pension. The maximum possible lump sum is reached after 20 years. The maximum rate of build up allowed is shown in Table 14 overleaf.

Table 14: Maximum pension and lump sum build up for pre-17 March 1987 schemes

Years of service	Pension as a fraction of final pay	Lump sum as a fraction of final pay
1	1/60	3/80
2	2/60	6/80
3	3/60	9/80
4	4/60	12/80
5	5/60	15/80
6	8/60	18/80
7	16/60	21/80
8	24/60	24/80
9	32/60	30/80
10	40/60	36/80
11		42/80
12		48/80
13		54/80
14		63/80
15		72/80
16		81/80
17		90/80
18		99/80
19		108/80
20		120/80

If you joined your scheme on or after 17 March 1987, you must have at least 20 years' membership, by retirement, in order to qualify for the maximum two-thirds pension. The fastest rate at which the pension can build up is one-thirtieth of final pay for each year. You need at least 20 years' service up to retirement to qualify for the maximum lump sum. If you joined your scheme on or after 17 March 1987, but before 1 June 1989 (unless you joined a new scheme which was set up on or after 14 March 1989), the rules regarding the rate at which the lump sum builds up are complicated – broadly, the proportion by which the lump sum has been boosted must match the proportion by which the pension has been boosted. If you joined your scheme on or after 1 June 1989, or you joined earlier but the scheme was set up on or after 14

March 1989, the lump sum must not exceed $2\frac{1}{4}$ times the maximum pension. In all these cases, the lump sum must not exceed $1\frac{1}{2}$ times final pay and must comply with the cash limits described in Table 13 on p. 65.

EXAMPLE

Chris became director of a finance company on 18 March 1987, and joined the pension scheme from that date. Suppose he stays until he reaches 65 by which time he has 20 years' service. By then, his final pay will be £30,000 (in today's money). The pension scheme is a generous one which will allow him to take a larger pension than a straight 'sixtieths' formula would allow. If the scheme paid one-sixtieth of his final pay for each year of membership, he would qualify for a pension of $\frac{1}{60} \times 20 \times £30,000 = £10,000$. The Inland Revenue rules allow a faster rate of pension build-up, and the maximum pension these rules allow would be one-thirtieth of final pay for each year, up to a maximum pension of two-thirds of final pay. This gives Chris a maximum possible pension of $\frac{2}{3} \times £30,000 = £20,000$.

The maximum boost – in the jargon, 'uplift' – to his pension is £20,000 – £10,000 = £10,000. In practice, the scheme is not quite so generous. It allows him to take a pension of £15,000. So the actual uplift is £5000/£10,000 = $\frac{1}{2}$ of the maximum uplift allowed by the tax rules.

If the lump sum he can take had built up according to the ordinary rules, the most he could have would be three-eightieths of his final pay for each year of service. This would come to $\frac{3}{80} \times 20 \times £30,000 = £22,500$. But the tax rules allow him more than this: referring to the pre-17 March 1987 table opposite, the maximum lump sum after 20 years service would be $1\frac{1}{2}$ times final pay – in other words £45,000. This would give a maximum possible uplift of £45,000 – £22,500 = £22,500. But his actual pension was boosted by only one-half of the maximum possible uplift. The tax rules require that his lump sum is boosted only by the same fraction. Thus, the maximum lump sum Chris can have is £22,500 + ($\frac{1}{2}$ × £22,500) = £33,750.

The Inland Revenue limits apply to nearly all types of employers' schemes – even money purchase schemes. Where the pension build-up rate exceeds sixtieths of final pay for each year of service, the maximum two-thirds-of-final-pay pension limit applies after taking account of any pensions you'll get from pension schemes and plans you've built up in the past – not just the pension from your current employer's scheme.

When is your employer's pension paid?

Your employer's scheme will have a **normal pension age**. Often this is the same as the state pension ages of 65 for men and 60 for women, but the scheme rules can set different ages.

At present, the majority of employers' schemes have a lower normal pension age for women than for men. Women can't be legally required to retire earlier than men, but British law does allow different pension ages for men and women – though such discrimination probably contravenes European Community law. If you're a woman who works on beyond the normal pension age for your scheme, you'll usually cease to build up pension benefits. Instead, your pension will either be increased to reflect your later retirement or, less commonly, it might start to be paid even though you're still working.

The tax rules prevent the maximum possible pensions being paid at very early ages. For a scheme which you joined before 1 June 1989, or a scheme which was set up before 14 March 1989, the maximum pension can't usually be paid before age 60 (men) or 55 (women). For a scheme you joined on or after 1 June 1989, or a scheme set up on or after 14 March 1989, the lowest age at which full pensions can be paid is 50. There are exceptions: for example, people in certain professions – such as divers or professional footballers – can retire earlier with a full pension. Special rules apply if you have to retire early due to ill health (see Chapter 10).

What do you pay?

Some employers' schemes are **non-contributory**. This means that your employer pays the whole cost of the scheme and you contribute nothing. The majority of schemes, however, are **contributory**, which means that you pay part of the cost and your employer pays part. Usually, you pay a given proportion of your salary into the scheme, say, five per cent.

With money purchase schemes, your employer will also pay a specified amount or percentage of your salary. But with final pay schemes (and similar schemes), the employer will provide however much is needed to make up the balance of the cost of providing the pensions and other benefits.

Both you and your employer get tax relief on contributions to an employer's scheme. Tax relief on your contributions is given by deducting them from your pay before your tax bill is worked out, and you get relief up to your highest rate of tax.

EXAMPLE

Megan earns £16,000 a year working for a bank and is a member of the pension scheme. The bank pays most of the cost of the scheme, but Megan contributes three per cent of her pay which comes to £480 a year. However, the cost to Megan is less than this because she gets tax relief on the contributions. As she pays tax at the basic rate of 25 per cent, the after-tax-relief cost of the contributions is only £360. (You can work it out like this: £480 × [1 − 0.25] = £360.)

The Inland Revenue limits the amount you can contribute to an employer's scheme. The limit is 15 per cent of your earnings. If you joined your scheme before 1 June 1989 and the scheme was set up before 14 March 1989, there's no other limit on the amount you can contribute. But, if you joined on or after 1 June 1989, or the scheme was newly set up on or after 14 March 1989, there's also an overall cash limit on the amount which can qualify for tax relief. In the 1990–91 tax year, this limit was £9,720. The cash limit will be increased each year in line with inflation as measured by changes in the Retail Prices Index. Table 15 below gives some examples of how much you can pay into an employer's pension scheme, depending on the amount you earn. There's no Inland

Table 15: The most you can pay into a pension scheme

Yearly earnings [1]	Maximum yearly contributions	After-tax-relief cost of contributions	
		25% taxpayer	40% taxpayer
£	£	£	£
10,000	1,500	1,125	900
15,000	2,250	1,688	1,350
20,000	3,000	2,250	1,800
25,000	3,750	2,813	2,250
30,000	4,500	3,375	2,700
40,000	6,000	[2]	3,600
50,000	7,500	[2]	4,500
60,000	9,000	[2]	5,400
70,000	10,500 [3]	[2]	6,300 [3]
80,000	12,000 [3]	[2]	7,200 [3]

[1] Including the taxable value of most fringe benefits
[2] Unlikely to be applicable
[3] If you joined scheme on or after 1 June 1989 or it was set up on or after 14 March 1989, maximum contribution in 1989–90 tax year is £9,000, which costs a 40% taxpayer £5,400

Revenue limit on the amount your employer can pay into a scheme as such, though there are rules to prevent him paying in more than is needed to provide the maximum possible benefits.

Too little pension?

As long as your total contributions remain within the tax limits, you can make extra pension contributions in order to boost your eventual pension. You can also use extra contributions to boost other benefits, such as pensions for dependants (see Chapter 9) or increases to your pension once it's being paid. But extra contributions which you start to pay on or after 17 March 1987 can't usually be used to provide or increase a tax-free lump sum.

Extra contributions are called **Additional Voluntary Contributions (AVCs)**. You can pay them either to an AVC scheme set up by your employer – all employers' schemes must have an AVC facility – or to your own **free-standing AVC (FSAVC) scheme**, which is a scheme independent of your employer's pension arrangements.

Many employers' AVC schemes, and all FSAVC schemes, work on a money purchase basis – in other words, your contributions are invested and build up a cash fund which is used at retirement to provide pension or other benefits. Some employers with final pay pension schemes have AVC schemes which work in a different way: your contributions are used to 'buy' extra years in the scheme. This has the effect of increasing your pension and any other benefits (including tax-free lump sums) which are based on your years of membership.

EXAMPLE

Peggy went back to work as a teacher after taking a number of years off to bring up her three children. She's belonged to the pension scheme for 16 years, and will have 21 years in the scheme by the time she reaches normal retirement age. In order to increase her eventual pension, Peggy is making AVCs into her employer's scheme. These 'buy' her extra years of membership, so that by retirement she will be credited with 25 years membership instead of 21. This will increase her pension by approximately £1,000 in terms of today's money – and the extra pension is guaranteed to increase in line with inflation once it's being paid.

You can't use AVCs to boost your pension or other benefits beyond the Inland Revenue limits (see p. 64). In the past, if you'd paid more in AVCs than was needed to bring your pension and other benefits up to the maximum level, the 'excess AVCs' were wasted. For schemes set up from 27 July 1989 onwards, any excess AVCs must be repaid at retirement, after tax, at a special rate of 35 per cent, has been deducted. Schemes set up before 27 July 1989 can also repay excess AVCs, but they can't be forced to do so. You can't reclaim the tax deducted from a refund of AVCs, and if you're a higher rate taxpayer you'll be required to pay some extra tax on the refund (see p. 195).

Executive schemes and small self-administered schemes

Executive schemes are special pension schemes designed for a small number of members – for example, an individual manager, or a group of directors. If you're a high-flier, your employer might operate such a scheme to cover you. They are also a possible choice if you run your own business as a company. Executive schemes are bound by the same rules as other employers' schemes – so the benefit and contribution limits outlined in this chapter apply. But the way they work is more like a personal plan: they are offered by investment and insurance companies who invest your contributions to build up a fund which will provide your pension benefits. The scheme provider charges you for administration and management of the investments.

Small self-administered schemes (SSAS) are small employers' schemes – usually with fewer than 12 members and most often used to provide pensions, and other benefits, for high-fliers and/or executives within a company. They can be a good choice for family-run companies with sufficient resources. SSASs are administered by investment or insurance companies. But the SSAS provider doesn't usually manage your investments itself. Instead, you have a wide choice about who will manage your money and how it will be invested. But this introduces an extra tier of management charges and makes these schemes unrealistic unless there is available around £100,000 or more to invest. Like executive schemes, SSASs are bound by the normal rules for employers' schemes, but the Inland Revenue also requires strict supervision of the membership and investments of a SSAS, including the appointment of a special trustee (see p. 76).

In the past, SSASs have been popular with small businesses, particularly because they provided a route for investing in the business's own premises or other property and a means of making loans to the business. At the time of writing, the government is introducing new laws which aim to stop all pension schemes and plans investing more than five per cent of their money in the parent company – either in the company's property, or by way of loans. SSASs will be exempt from this restriction as long as they meet certain conditions, such as: all members must also be trustees (see p. 76) and all decisions made by the trustees must be unanimous.

More information

If your employer runs a pension scheme which you are eligible to join, you must be given basic information about the scheme if you request it – many schemes will automatically give you these details. Once you are a member, you must be given a booklet explaining how the scheme works. You're entitled to receive a **benefit statement** giving you details about the benefits you're building up with a scheme – sometimes you need to ask for these statements but, with many schemes, benefit statements are issued automatically once a year. As a member, you're also entitled to inspect the documents relating to the setting up of the scheme and to see the annual trustees' report and the scheme accounts. Many schemes now circulate an abbreviated version of the report and accounts to the members, or draw attention to their availability.

Your main source of additional information about your employer's pension scheme is the scheme officials or your personnel department at work. The scheme officials are usually the pensions administrator and the trustees of the scheme (see appendix to this chapter). These are also the people you should go to initially if you have a problem.

If you can't resolve a difficulty through direct contact with the scheme officials, you could turn to the Occupational Pensions Advisory Service (OPAS) for help. OPAS will not make any judgment in a disputed case, but they will investigate what your rights are, explain these to you, help you put your case to the scheme, and if necessary contact the scheme for you. You can get in touch with OPAS either through your local Citizens Advice Bureau (CAB) – their address and telephone number are in the telephone book – or by contacting the service direct (address on p. 214). If you require general information about pension schemes – but not advice or help in specific cases – you could contact the Pensions Information Manager at the Association of British Insurers (address on p. 213).

At the time of writing, the government is introducing new laws which will set up a Pensions Ombudsman to investigate and determine cases where you think you have suffered injustice because of maladministration by your pension scheme. As yet, details of how you will be able to contact the Ombudsman are not available.

APPENDIX TO CHAPTER 5

How pension schemes are organised

Qualifying for tax relief

An employer's pension scheme will qualify for the tax reliefs described in this chapter (see p. 58) only if it is *approved* by the Inland Revenue. An essential requirement for approval is that the assets of the pension scheme are kept quite separate from the employer's business. This separation may be achieved by setting up a **statutory scheme** – in other words, a scheme set up under an Act of Parliament. Statutory schemes are found in the public sector covering, for example, teachers, and local and central government employees.

In the private sector, the separation of the pension scheme from the employer is usually achieved by setting up a **trust**. A trust is a legal arrangement which puts specified assets into the hands of one or more **trustees**. They are required to look after the assets and use them for the benefit of a specified person or group of people who are called the **beneficiaries** of the trust. The purpose of the trust and the particular rules that the trustees must follow will be set out in the **trust deed and rules**.

A pension scheme trust

In the case of a pension scheme, the purpose of the trust is to provide pensions and other benefits for the members of the scheme. The assets which are handed over to the trust are the contributions made by the employer, and those of the employees if it is a contributory scheme, possibly some money from the government, and the investment income and capital growth from investing these amounts. The beneficiaries of the scheme are current employees who belong to the scheme, past employees who've left but still have a right to a pension from the scheme when they reach retirement, past employees who have retired and are now receiving pensions from the scheme, and the dependants of the scheme members who may be entitled to a pension or lump sum from the scheme in the event of a member's death.

The trustees

The trustees of a scheme can be organised in a number of ways:

- **individual trustees** A number of individuals are appointed, each of whom is a trustee. They meet as a group to take decisions, and one of them is usually elected as a chairman
- **corporate trustee** A special company is formed to take on the role of trustee. Individuals are elected as directors of the company, and it's the Board of Directors which takes the decisions. The directors probably have the same responsibilities as they would if they were individual trustees, though this is a grey area of the law
- **professional trustee** A pension scheme can employ an outside specialist to act as trustee. This might be, for example, a bank or insurance company with a department or subsidiary which specialises in trustee work
- **pensioneer trustee** A small self-administered pension scheme (see p. 73) must have as its trustee, or as one of its trustees, a professional who is approved by the Inland Revenue and who is called a pensioneer trustee. As well as the normal duties of a trustee, a pensioneer trustee has a duty to the Inland Revenue to guard against the pension scheme being improperly used for the benefit of the employer

- **the employer**   The employer can be the sole trustee of the scheme, though this is fairly unusual.

The trustees may be appointed by the employer, but this need not be so. A board of individual trustees may be made up of managers, employees and pensioners, and the employee trustees will often have been selected by a trade union or elected by the employee members of the scheme. However they are appointed, trustees are under a duty to run the scheme (in accordance with the trust deed and rules) strictly for the benefit of the members; the trustees are not representatives of any particular group – such as management or the union – and should never act as if they are.

Though the trustees are ultimately responsible for the running of the pension scheme, they can employ help – for example, they must appoint an administrator to handle the day-to-day business of the scheme, they may employ a specialist to advise on the scheme's investment policy or to manage the investments. They will need the services of an actuary periodically to evaluate the scheme.

═6═

PERSONAL PENSION PLANS

Personal pension plans are a way of making your own pension arrangements by saving with an insurance company, unit trust, building society, bank or friendly society. The organisation with which you save – here, called the **plan provider** – invests your money to build up a cash fund. At retirement, the fund is used to provide your pension.

Personal pension plans can be used for contracting out of the State Earnings Related Pension Scheme (SERPS) – this aspect of the plans is dealt with in Chapter 7.

Who qualifies?

Anybody who is at least age 16 and under the age of 75 with earnings can take out a personal pension plan. You can't simultaneously belong to an employer's pension scheme and pay into a personal plan (unless it's a personal plan used solely for contracting out of SERPS). This means that many employees will have to choose whether to be a member of their employer's scheme or to contribute to their own personal plan instead. A good employer's scheme is expensive to replace, so think carefully before opting for a personal plan.

If you're self-employed, you have to make your own provision for retirement, and personal pension plans will generally be the best way of doing this. If you run your own business as a company, a personal pension plan is one way in which you can save for retirement, but you might instead set up your own employer's scheme (see p. 72).

Subject to the contribution limits (see p. 84), you can generally contribute to more than one personal pension plan at a time.

How much pension?

All personal pension plans work on a **money purchase** basis (see p. 60). This means that you can't, in advance, be sure of how much pension you'll get. The pension will depend on the amount you contribute, how the invested contributions grow, and the rate – **annuity rate** – at which your cash fund can be exchanged for pension at the time you retire. You have a choice about how your savings are invested – you'll find details in Chapter 11.

A personal plan can also provide benefits for your dependants, such as pensions for a widow or widower, or children (see Chapter 9). Using the plan to provide dependants' benefits reduces the amount to be used for your retirement pension. Similarly, you 'pay' extra (by receiving a lower pension at the start of your retirement) for a pension which increases after retirement – for example, by a fixed amount each year, or by enough to match inflation.

Tax-free cash at retirement

As with employers' pension schemes, you can usually take part of the proceeds from a personal pension plan as a tax-free lump sum at retirement. Doing this obviously reduces the amount of pension you get, but generally taking the cash is worthwhile. If you can't manage on the reduced pension, you could use your tax-free cash to buy a **purchased life annuity**. As described on p. 63, the after-tax income from a purchased life annuity is likely to exceed the after-tax amount of pension which you give up in order to take the tax-free cash. How much tax-free cash you can have depends on the type of personal pension plan that you have and when you first started it. The limits are shown in Table 16 overleaf.

Table 16: How much tax-free cash you can have

Type of plan and when started	Maximum amount of tax-free cash
Old-style personal pension plans [1] (called retirement annuity contracts, section 620 plans or section 226 plans)	
Started before 17 March 1987	Three times the remaining pension
Started on or after 17 March 1987 and before 1 July 1988	Three times the remaining pension up to an overall maximum of £150,000
New-style personal pension plans [1]	
Started on or after 1 July 1988 and before 27 July 1989	One-quarter of pension fund (except amounts to be used to provide dependants' pensions) up to an overall maximum of £150,000
Started on or after 27 July 1989	One-quarter of pension fund (except amounts to be used to provide 'contracted-out' [2] pensions) without any overall maximum

[1] Old-style plans were available before 1 July 1988. Since then, only new-style plans have been allowed to be started. You can continue to save using an old-style plan if you already have one
[2] See Chapter 7

EXAMPLE

Iain is about retire. He has an old-style personal pension plan to which he has contributed for over 20 years. He can either take a pension from the plan of £9,300 a year, or he can take a lower pension and up to £21,000 as a tax-free lump sum. If he takes the maximum lump sum, his pension will be reduced to £7,000 a year.

EXAMPLE

Jack is saving for retirement using a new-style personal pension plan. If, by retirement, he builds up a fund of £143,000 (in terms of today's money), he could choose to take up to one-quarter of the fund – in other words, £35,750 – as a tax-free lump sum. If he did this, he'd be left with a pension of £11,250 a year instead of a full pension of £15,000 a year.

When is the pension paid?

You don't have to stop work in order to take a pension from a personal plan. However, the Inland Revenue lays down rules which prevent you taking your pension too early in life. With old-style personal plans – plans taken out before 1 July 1988 – you normally can't start to take your pension before you reach age 60. There are some exceptions – for example, if you have to retire through ill-health (see Chapter 10), or if you have an occupation for which an earlier retirement age has been officially recognised (see Table 17 overleaf).

With new-style personal plans – those taken out on or after 1 July 1988 – the rules allow you to take your pension from age 50 onwards, so for many of the occupations listed in Table 17, there's no need for special treatment. But the special retirement ages of 35, 40 and 45 apply to the occupations as shown in the case of new-style, as well as old-style, plans.

Inland Revenue rules prohibit you from paying into either a new-style or an old-style personal pension plan after reaching age 75, and that is the latest age at which you can start to draw your pension. Within the Inland Revenue age limits, the organisation providing the plan may have its own rules about the normal pension age. It's rare that a plan has a single fixed pension age. With some plans, you choose your own retirement age at the time you first take out the plan, though you may be able to change your mind later on. Other plans are even more flexible, and let you leave your decision until you're ready to start taking the pension. You can increase your scope for

Table 17: Occupations with early retirement ages

Age	Occupation	Age	Occupation
35	Athletes	50	Croupiers
	Badminton players		Martial arts instructors
	Boxers		Money broker dealers
	Cyclists		Newscasters
	Dancers		Offshore riggers
	Footballers		Royal Navy Reservists
	Models		Rugby League referees
	National Hunt jockeys		Territorial Army
	Rugby League players		members
	Squash players	55	Air pilots
	Table tennis players		Brass instrumentalists
	Tennis players		Distant water trawlermen
	Wrestlers		In-shore fishermen
40	Cricketers		Money broker dealer
	Golfers		directors
	Motor cycle riders		Nurses, midwives etc
	Motor racing drivers		National Health Service
	Speedway riders		psychiatrists
	Trapeze artists		Part-time firemen
	Divers		Singers
45	Flat-racing jockeys		
	Non-commissioned Royal		
	Marine Reservists		

flexibility by having several pension plans and starting your pension from each at a different age. For example, you might have four plans with pension ages of 60, 61, 62 and 65.

The later you start taking your pension, the longer your pension fund is left invested and, usually, the longer you carry on making contributions. Since you'll be older when the pension starts (and your life expectancy will be lower – see p. 9), the pension provider can expect to pay out the pension for a shorter period. This means that your pension is likely to be greater the later you start receiving it. Conversely, if you retire early, you'll generally have to make do with a smaller pension.

What do you pay?

You can choose whether to take out a plan (sometimes called a **regular premium** plan) which requires regular payments – for example, monthly or yearly – or a plan which requires only a single lump sum contribution (sometimes called a **single premium** pension plan). There may be a minimum contribution – for example, £20 a month or £200 a year with a regular payment plan, or £1,000 with a lump sum plan.

Most regular payment plans let you increase your contributions – either by a fixed amount each year, or in line with price or earnings inflation. Increases may be automatic, or optional. Generally, you should consider increasing your payments regularly, so that your pension savings don't fall back in terms of today's money. You may also be able to make extra one-off payments to your regular payment plan.

Many regular payment plans also allow you to reduce your payments, or miss a limited number of payments without penalty – though you may have to pay extra for this option. Chapter 11 looks, among other things, at the pros and cons of regular payment plans versus lump sum plans.

Tax relief on your savings

You get tax relief up to your highest rate of income tax on the amount you contribute to a personal pension plan. This means, for example, that a taxpayer paying tax at a 25 per cent rate can contribute £100 to a plan at a cost of only £75. The cost to a 40 per cent taxpayer of contributing £100 would be only £60 after tax relief.

With new-style personal plans (in other words, plans taken out on or after 1 July 1988), if you work for an employer you get basic rate tax relief automatically by paying only the after-tax-relief amount into your plan. If you're a higher rate taxpayer, you have to claim the extra tax relief due to you. If you're self-employed, you make full before-tax-relief payments to your plan provider and must claim through your tax office all the tax relief due to you.

With old-style pension plans (those taken out before 1 July 1988), all payments are made before taking account of tax relief. You have to claim the tax relief due to you. You can make a ' claim for tax relief on your personal pension contributions either through your Tax Return, or by using Form PP120 which you can get from your tax office.

EXAMPLE

Ryan is 45 and finance director of a small knitwear firm. In the 1989–90 tax year he contributed £8,500 (before tax relief) to his new-style personal pension plan. He received basic rate tax relief of £2,125 (25 per cent of £8,500) automatically, so he handed over £6,375 to the insurance company which runs his plan. But Ryan pays higher rate tax of 40 per cent on at least £8,500 of his income, so he can claim additional tax relief of £1,275 (40 per cent of £8,500 less the basic rate tax relief already given). The total after-tax-relief cost to him of the £8,500 contribution is only £5,100 (£8,500 less basic rate relief of £2,125 and less higher rate relief of £1,275).

Limits on what you pay

The Inland Revenue limits the amount of pension contributions you can make which will qualify for tax relief. The limits vary according to your age and the type of personal plan. They are set as a percentage of your **net relevant earnings**. If you're an employee, this means your total before-tax pay including the value of most taxable fringe benefits (for example, a company car, or cheap loan). If you're self-employed, net relevant earnings basically means your profits for tax purposes. The limits tell you the maximum **before-tax-relief** amount that you can pay into your personal plan.

Table 18 opposite shows the contribution limits for new-style personal plans.

Table 18: Tax-relief limits on contributions to new-style pension plans [1]

Your age at the start of the tax year (6 april)	Amount of relief as a percentage of your earnings	Amount of relief in £££ for each £1,000 of your earnings
Up to 35	17.5%	£175
36 to 45	20%	£200
46 to 50	25%	£250
51 to 55	30%	£300
56 to 60	35%	£350
61 to 74	40%	£400
75 and over	you can no longer contribute	

[1] Personal pension plans taken out on or after 1 July 1988

In addition to the percentages listed above, there is an overall cash limit on the amount of earnings which can be taken into account in working out your contribution limit. In the 1990–91 tax year, the earnings limit is £64,800. This means, for example, that someone aged 30 earning £70,000 can contribute at most 17.5 per cent of £64,800 which comes to £11,340. The earnings limit will be increased each year in line with changes in the Retail Prices Index.

If you're an employee, your employer can contribute to a new-style personal pension plan on your behalf, but the amount he pays counts towards your contribution limit. If you're using a personal pension plan to contract out of SERPS (see Chapter 7), amounts used for contracting out don't count towards the contribution limit.

Table 19, overleaf, shows the contribution limits which apply to old-style personal plans.

If you're an employee, your employer can't contribute to an old-style personal plan, and these plans can't be used for contracting-out. Unlike new-style plans, there is no cash limit on the amount which you can pay into an old-style personal pension plan. Despite this, unless their earnings are high,

Table 19: Tax-relief limits on contributions to old-style personal plans [1]

Age at the start of the tax year (6 April)	Amount of relief as a percentage of your earnings	Amount of relief in £££ for each £1,000 of your earnings
Up to 50	17.5%	£175
51 to 55	20%	£200
56 to 60	22.5%	£225
61 to 74	27.5%	£275
75 and over	you can no longer contribute	

[1] Personal pension plans taken out before 1 July 1988

anyone over 35 will be able to pay more into a new-style plan than an old-style one because the percentage limits for new-style plans are higher. At the 1990–91 cash limit, you'll be able to contribute more to an old-style plan than a new-style one only if your earnings exceed the limits in Table 20 below.

It's possible for you to be paying into new- and old-style plans at the same time. In this situation, the tax-relief limits for

Table 20: Maximising your contributions: old- or new-style plan?

Age at the start of the tax year (6 April)	Earnings above which maximum contributions to an old-style personal plan may exceed those to a new-style plan [1]
36 to 45	£74,057
46 to 50	£92,571
51 to 55	£97,200
56 to 60	£100,800
61 to 74	£94,255

[1] Based on 1990–91 contribution limits

each type of plan apply, but in addition your total contributions to all your plans usually must not exceed the new-style plan limit – see the example below.

EXAMPLE

Leonard saves for retirement mainly through an old-style personal pension plan which he took out back in 1956 (when old-style plans were first launched). He also started a new-style plan in July 1988. Leonard is 62 now and wants to contribute as much as possible to his plans to boost his income once he retires. His earnings in the 1990–91 tax year are £43,000. He can contribute up to 27.5 per cent of £43,000 = £11,825 to his old-style plan. He can contribute up to 40 per cent of £43,000 = £17,200 to his new-style plan. But his total contributions to both plans can't exceed the new-style plan limit – in other words, £17,200. He decides to pay the full £11,825 into his old-style plan, which lets him pay up to £17,200 – £11,825 = £5,375 into his new-style plan.

Going over the tax relief

In general, if you pay more into a new-style personal pension plan than the tax relief rules allow, your excess contributions will be returned to you as soon as the over-payment is spotted. If you're an employee and both you and your employer contribute to the plan, any over-payment will be repaid to you rather than your employer. Excess contributions to an old-style plan may be left invested but they'll be treated as an ordinary investment and won't qualify for the special tax treatment given to pension plans.

However, there are two situations in which you can make contributions which do come to more than your tax relief limit for a particular tax year. The first is where you use the **carry back** rule. This allows you to have a contribution that you pay in one tax year treated as if it had been paid in the previous year. You must have enough unused tax-relief limit for the previous year to cover the amount carried back. If you had no net relevant earnings in the previous year, you can carry back the contribution two years. In either case, you get tax relief at the rates which applied in the earlier tax year.

Carrying back contributions can be particularly useful if you're a higher rate taxpayer or self-employed, because you'll usually get the tax relief that you claim more quickly than you would with a contribution which is not carried back (because the relief arises from a revised tax assessment for the earlier year). At present, you won't lose out by carrying back a contribution but, if the tax climate alters, take care that you don't carry back to a year when tax rates were lower than in the current year. In a situation where the tax rate for the earlier year was higher than the rate for the current year, it would of course be advantageous to carry back a contribution.

EXAMPLE

Jean's a 50-year-old self-employed graphic designer. She generally pays £1,000 a year into her old-style personal pension plan. In the 1988–89 tax year, she earned more than usual and decided to put a bit more into her plan. Rather than increasing her contribution for that year, Jean asked for an extra £500 to be treated as if she'd paid it in the previous year. Not only did she get tax relief on the contribution within a couple of months, but she also received relief at the higher 27 per cent basic tax rate which applied during 1987–88 instead of the 25 per cent rate which applied in 1988–89.

The second way to contribute more than the current year's tax-relief limit allows is by using the **carry forward** rules. You can do this, if you have any unused tax-relief limit from the last six years. You can carry forward the unused relief, and use it now. You must carry forward from the earliest year first. But note that you get relief at the current tax rates – not the tax rates which applied in the earlier years.

Different tax relief limits applied for the years 1982–83 to 1986–87, and they were based on the year in which you were born, rather than your age at the start of the tax year as now. Table 21 shows the limits which applied in these earlier years.

Table 21: Tax relief limits on contributions to old-style personal plans for the years 1982–83 to 1986–87

Year of birth	Amount of relief as a percentage of earnings	Amount of relief in £££ for each £1,000 of earnings
1934 or later	17.5%	£175
1916 to 1933	20%	£200
1914 to 1915	21%	£210
1912 to 1913	24%	£240
1910 to 1911	26.5%	£265
1908 to 1909	29.5%	£295

EXAMPLE

Jean (aged 50) had another good year in 1989–90. She landed a very lucrative contract for an American firm which more than doubled her normal yearly earnings. She decided to put a large part of the extra money into her pension plan, though this took her over the tax-relief limit for that year. But she was able to use previously unused relief from earlier years. Table 22 overleaf shows Jean's earnings and tax-relief limits for 1989–90 and the preceding six years.

Jean puts £6,500 into her pension plan in the 1989–90 tax year. This uses up her whole tax relief limit for that year plus £3,420 of relief from earlier years. This uses up all the relief from 1983–84 up to 1987–88, but still leaves £350 unused relief from 1988–89. She can continue to carry this £350 relief forward.

89

Table 22: Jean's earnings and tax-relief limits

Tax year	Jean's earnings	Pension tax-relief limit	Jean's contributions	Unused relief for the year
1989–90	£17,600	£3,080	£6,500	£ 0
1988–89	£11,800	£2,065	£1,000	£1,065
1987–88	£ 9,600	£1,680	£1,500	£ 180
1986–87	£ 9,000	£1,575	£1,000	£ 575
1985–86	£ 9,200	£1,610	£1,000	£ 610
1984–85	£ 8,600	£1,505	£ 800	£ 705
1983–84	£ 8,200	£1,435	£ 800	£ 635
			Total unused relief for previous six years:	£3,770

Special rules for doctors and dentists

If you're a GP or dentist working in a practice, you count as self-employed for tax purposes. But, unusually, you're eligible to contribute to what is, in effect, an employer's pension scheme – the National Health Service (NHS) Superannuation Scheme. *At the same time*, you can contribute to your own personal pension plan, and there are special rules to work out how much you can contribute to this. As a GP or dentist, you have a choice:

- you can pay into the NHS scheme but give up all tax relief on these contributions. In this case, all your earnings count as net relevant earnings (see p. 84); the tax-relief limit for personal plan contributions is then worked out in the normal way
- you can pay into the NHS scheme and receive tax relief as normal on these contributions. Multiplying the NHS scheme contribution by 16⅔ gives a figure for the earnings which are covered by that scheme. Subtracting this amount from your total earnings leaves the amount of net relevant earnings

which can be used as the basis of working out contributions to a personal plan.

If you're a dentist or a GP, you can, of course, decide not to join the NHS scheme at all – or to leave it if you already belong. In that case, you could use all your earnings as a basis for contributions to a personal plan in the normal way. But the NHS scheme is a good one and, in practice, you're likely to do better by joining it.

If you belong to the NHS scheme, you can make additional voluntary contributions (AVCs) – see p. 71 – as long as your total contributions don't exceed the normal limit applying to an employer's scheme, which is usually 15 per cent of your earnings. Your AVCs can be made either to the NHS AVC scheme or to a free-standing AVC scheme. If you do make AVCs, the rules for working out your possible contributions to a personal plan are more complicated than those outlined above.

EXAMPLE

Derek is a 31-year-old doctor earning £30,000 a year from a thriving group practice. In the 1990–91 tax year, he pays tax at the basic rate of 25 per cent. He pays £1,000 a year into the NHS scheme; this has a 6 per cent contribution rate, so multiplying by $16\frac{2}{3}$ gives a figure for the amount of Derek's earnings which are covered by the NHS scheme. This figure is £16,666. Derek would like to take out a personal pension plan as well. He has two options:

- he can receive tax relief of £250 (25 per cent of £1,000) on the contribution to the NHS scheme. This means that he'll have net relevant earnings of £30,000 − £16,666 = £13,334 which can be used as a basis of his contributions to a personal plan. The maximum contribution he could make would be £2,333 which would qualify for £583 tax relief. In total, he'd be contributing £3,333 to his pension savings with total tax relief of £833

- alternatively, Derek could give up the £250 tax relief on the NHS scheme contribution. In this case, his full £30,000 earnings would be eligible as a basis for contributions to a personal plan. His maximum contribution would be £5,250 which would qualify for tax relief of £1,313.

If Derek wants to make relatively large savings for retirement, the second option looks promising. But he should also consider whether he'd do better by making AVCs to the NHS scheme or a free-standing AVC scheme, instead of taking out a personal plan.

More information

Plan providers and pension advisers can give you details about particular pension plans, and may be able to help you make your pension choices – see Chapter 12 for details.

If you have a problem concerning a personal pension plan, which the plan provider or your adviser can't resolve, you could contact the Occupational Pensions Advisory Service (OPAS). Despite its name, OPAS now deals also with personal pensions. It does not make any judgements about disputes, but it can investigate your case and explain the facts to you. It can also contact the plan provider on your behalf. You can contact OPAS through Citizens Advice Bureaux, or direct (address on p. 214). If you require general information about personal plans, you could contact the Pensions Information Manager at the Association of British Insurers (address on p. 213). The Pensions Ombudsman (see p. 74) will be able to investigate cases relating to personal pension plan arrangements.

=7=

CONTRACTING OUT OF SERPS

If you're an employee earning more than a lower earnings limit (£46 a week in the 1990–91 tax year), you're eligible for the State Earnings Related Pension Scheme (SERPS). As a member of SERPS, at retirement, you'll receive a pension which is worked out according to a formula, and depends largely on the average of your earnings during your working life. Chapter 4 describes the scheme in detail. You can opt out of SERPS. This is called **contracting out**, which means that you give up some or all of the state earnings related pension and receive a pension from an employer's scheme or a personal plan instead.

How to contract out

Generally, you can choose whether or not to contract out. But if you're an employee belonging to a **contracted-out employer's scheme**, the choice has been made for you – the only way in which you could rejoin SERPS would be by leaving your employer's scheme. Usually, that would not be worth doing just for the sake of contracting back into SERPS.

If you belong to an employer's scheme which isn't contracted-out, there are several ways in which you can contract out – and you don't have to leave your employer's scheme. If you're not in an employer's scheme at all, you can contract out using a personal pension plan.

Chart 9 overleaf summarises your options.

Chart 9: How to contract out of SERPS

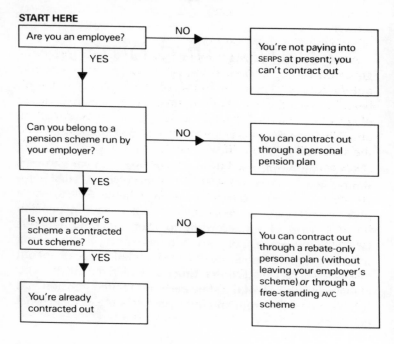

START HERE

Are you an employee? — NO → You're not paying into SERPS at present; you can't contract out

YES ↓

Can you belong to a pension scheme run by your employer? — NO → You can contract out through a personal pension plan

YES ↓

Is your employer's scheme a contracted out scheme? — NO → You can contract out through a rebate-only personal plan (without leaving your employer's scheme) *or* through a free-standing AVC scheme

YES ↓

You're already contracted out

How does contracting out work?

Employer's final pay schemes

If you're contracted out through your employer's final pay pension scheme (see p. 59), both you and your employer pay lower National Insurance on your earnings above the lower earnings limit. This reflects the fact that neither of you is contributing to SERPS during the period for which you're contracted out.

With a final pay scheme, contracting out means that the scheme guarantees to pay you a minimum amount of pension at retirement – a **guaranteed minimum pension (GMP).** (It will also pay a guaranteed widow's or widower's pension.) Your GMP will be broadly equal to the SERPS pension you'd otherwise have built up. But the precise amount of the GMP doesn't really matter because *you can't lose by contracting out through a final pay scheme*. This becomes clear once you look at what happens when you retire.

At retirement, the Department of Social Security (DSS) – the government department responsible for pensions – works out the full SERPS pension you would have got if you hadn't been contracted out at all. From this, it subtracts the amount of any GMPs you qualify for because of periods of contracting out. Whatever remains is the amount of SERPS pension which the state will pay you. (If your GMPs equal or exceed the full SERPS pension, you'll get no SERPS pension.) If your GMPs are large, you'll receive only a small SERPS pension; if your GMPs are small, you'll receive a larger SERPS pension. But the GMPs plus the SERPS pension you're paid will together always equal the maximum SERPS pension you could have got without contracting out.

You can't lose by contracting out this way and, in practice, you're likely to gain, because most employer's schemes aim to provide a pension which is greater than just the GMP. You may or may not be required to contribute to the scheme to pay towards the GMP and any extra pension or other benefits.

EXAMPLE

Alfred (see p. 52) retired late in 1988 with a SERPS pension of £14.04 week – £730 a year. Henry is Alfred's twin brother, and in one of those extraordinary coincidences that seem to afflict twins, his yearly earnings were identical to Alfred's during the last few years before retirement. However, unlike Alfred, Henry was contracted into SERPS only for the last two years that he worked. For three years before that, he belonged to a contracted-out final pay scheme (and, before that, he and Alfred ran a small business together). The final pay scheme now pays Henry a GMP of £435 a year. This is subtracted from the SERPS pension of £730 a year which he would have had if he'd never been contracted out. The remaining £295 (£730 less £435) is the amount of SERPS pension which he received at retirement. The SERPS pension he gets is increased each year to reflect the effect of inflation on his whole pension (SERPS pension plus GMP) – see p. 99.

Employer's money purchase schemes

Contracting out through an employer's money purchase scheme (see p. 60) – sometimes called a **COMP** – works quite differently. You and your employer still both pay lower National Insurance on your earnings above the lower earnings limit. But the employer's scheme doesn't make any guarantees about the amount of pension it will pay you to replace the SERPS you'd otherwise have been building up. Instead, your employer is required to guarantee that he will pay a set amount into the scheme which will be left to build up a fund. The amount invested is equal to the amounts that you and your employer have saved by paying lower National Insurance – it is called the **rebate**. The fund which builds up must be used to provide you a retirement pension (and a widow's or widower's pension). Your rights to these benefits are called your **protected rights**. How much the protected rights pension will be depends on how well the invested money grows and on the rate – the **annuity rate** – at which the fund can be converted to pension when the time comes for it to be paid.

At retirement, the DSS again works out the full SERPS pension you would have built up if you'd not been contracted out at all. But then, it subtracts the amount of the GMP you would have built up, if during the period you were contracted out, you'd belonged to a contracted-out final pay scheme. This is called a **notional GMP** and it may be more or less than the actual pension that you receive from the contracted-out money purchase scheme.

If your invested fund grows well and annuity rates are favourable when you come to retire, contracting out through an employer's money purchase scheme may mean that you end up with more pension than you would have done had you stayed in SERPS. But, if your invested fund does badly and annuity rates are low when you retire, you may find with hindsight that you'd have been better off staying in SERPS. You take a gamble (though the gamble will be small in some cases – see p. 103).

A contracted-out money purchase scheme can be designed to accept contributions paid by your employer, as well as just the rebate, and your employer may or may not require you to make contributions too.

EXAMPLE

Jacky is 25. She has just started work as a receptionist with a firm of office equipment suppliers on a salary of £12,000 a year. The firm has recently set up a contracted-out money purchase (COMP) pension scheme which Jacky has decided to join. Until now, she's made no savings for retirement apart from contributions to the state basic and SERPS pensions through paying National Insurance.

To work out whether Jacky's decision is a good one, various assumptions need to be made about her future earnings, future investment returns and future annuity rates. Suppose that by contracting out in the 1990–91 tax year, Jacky gives up £45 a year (in today's money) of her eventual SERPS pension. On modest assumptions, the COMP scheme might provide a pension at retirement of, say, £140 a year. Clearly, contracting out through the COMP scheme is a good idea for Jacky in 1990–91. She should review the situation every year.

Personal pension plans

If you contract out through a personal pension plan – called an **appropriate personal pension** – you and your employer carry on paying National Insurance at the full rate on all your earnings, but the DSS repays part of it – called the **rebate** – which is paid directly into your personal pension plan. The rebate is invested to build up a fund which will be used to provide you with a retirement pension (and a widow's or widower's pension) in place of the SERPS pension you'd otherwise have built up. Your rights to these benefits are called your **protected rights**. The amount of protected rights pension your plan provides depends on how well the invested rebate grows and annuity rates at the time you retire.

As with contracting out through an employer's money purchase scheme, at retirement the DSS works out the full SERPS pension that you could have built up and then subtracts notional GMPs corresponding to periods when you were contracted out. Depending on how well your personal plan has performed, the notional GMPs may be greater or smaller than the actual pension your plan provides. Once again, contracting out means that you could end up with more or with less pension than if you'd stayed in SERPS.

An appropriate personal pension is technically a single lump sum contribution plan which may accept only the amount of the rebate, any incentive (see p. 102) and any related tax relief (see p. 105). If you belong to an employer's pension scheme, and simultaneously contract out using a personal plan, you can only have an appropriate pension plan – called a **rebate only plan** or **minimum appropriate personal pension**. But, if you don't belong to an employer's scheme, your appropriate plan can form part of a personal pension plan package which receives contributions greater than just the rebate.

Free-standing AVC schemes

If you belong to an employer's scheme, you can contract out using a free-standing additional voluntary contribution (FSAVC) scheme (see p. 71), instead of a personal pension plan. But, in practice, you'll always do better to choose the personal pension plan route, because a quirk in the tax rules (see p. 106) means that the DSS pays less into a contracted-out free-standing AVC scheme than it pays into a contracted-out personal plan.

EXAMPLE

Jonathan belongs to a contracted-in employer's pension scheme. If he wished, he could contract out through either a personal pension plan or a free-standing AVC scheme. In the 1990–91 tax year, the government would pay a total of £1,338 into a personal pension plan that he took out, but only £1,233 into a free-standing AVC scheme. The difference represents the tax relief available on the rebate paid into the personal plan, but not available on the rebate paid into the FSAVC scheme.

After retirement

SERPS pensions are increased each year in line with changes in the Retail Prices Index. If you're contracted out, the state used to continue to provide the full increase required to keep your SERPS and GMPs growing in line with inflation. But this has now changed: the scheme providing a contracted-out pension, or the plan provider, must increase the pension at a rate of three per cent a year, or by the rate of inflation if this is less. This change affects employers' pensions for people retiring on or after 6 April 1990, but only for GMPs built up since 6 April 1988. It affects personal pensions built up from 1 July 1988 onwards.

Each year, the DSS recalculates the amount of SERPS it must pay you by subtracting your GMPs or notional GMPs from the full SERPS pension that you could theoretically have built up. But the figures used in the calculation will have been revised to take account of the inflation-proofing. The full SERPS pension will have been increased in line with the change in the Retail Prices Index. The GMPs and notional GMPs will have been increased each time by three per cent a year. The result of these yearly revisions is that, if contracting out left you at the start of retirement with a lower pension than you'd otherwise have got, the shortfall will increase year by year. But, if contracting out left you better off, the excess will increase each year.

Should you contract out?

SERPS provides a pension which is linked to your earnings and keeps pace with changes in national earnings up to retirement and with changes in prices after retirement. If you're contracted out through an employer's final pay scheme, you lose none of this and it makes little odds whether you're in SERPS or out. But, if the final pay route isn't open to you, should you contract out? Is it worth giving up the security of SERPS for the opportunities, but uncertainties, of contracting out? The answer depends largely on four factors:

- your sex
- your age
- your view about future investment performance
- the size of the rebate.

Your sex

Men and women, on average, don't benefit equally from SERPS. The state pension age for women is 60; the pension age for men is 65. Also, a woman can expect to live some four or five years longer than a man of the same age now. So, supposing a man and a woman had an identical entitlement to SERPS at the start of their retirements, the woman could expect to receive her pension for about eight years longer than the man, and would thus receive considerably more pension overall.

Despite this difference in the total amount of pension a man and a woman can expect to receive, the rebate to be invested in a contracted-out employer's money purchase scheme or a personal plan is identical for a man and a woman who earn the same. Yet, other factors being equal, the woman is giving up more SERPS than the man. The upshot of this is that contracting out is more likely to be attractive to men than to women.

Your age

SERPS pension is worked out according to a formula, but a contracted-out money purchase pension – such as that provided by an employer's money purchase scheme or a personal plan – depends to a large extent on how the invested rebates grow. If you're young, you have a long time until you reach pension age: your rebates will be invested for longer, and can be expected to grow by more than the rebates of an older person who'll reach retirement sooner.

In addition, SERPS pensions are being cut back for people retiring after the end of this century. The cut-backs are being phased in gradually, with the result that the earlier you reach state pension age (in other words, the older you are), the more SERPS pension you would give up through contracting out, compared with a younger person. Since you receive the same rate of rebate regardless of age, contracting out is more attractive the younger you are.

Your view about future investment performance

With contracted-out money purchase pensions, investment performance will play a large part in determining how large or small your eventual pension will be. If you're optimistic on this score, and expect your invested rebates to grow well, contracting out will tend to be an attractive option. If, on the other hand, you take a more cautious view of likely investment growth, you'll be more attracted to staying in SERPS.

101

The size of the rebate

The size of the rebate is set by the government on the advice of its actuary. (An actuary is a professional whose skills lie in assessing probabilities and likely future values from statistical and other data.) The amount of the rebate is supposed roughly to represent the cost of buying a GMP for an average member of a large employer's final pay scheme. The rebate is reviewed every five years; the next review is due in 1993 and the rebate is expected to be reduced then from its current level. In each of the years from 6 April 1988 to 5 April 1993, the rebate equals 5.8 per cent of your earnings between the lower and upper earnings limits. Two per cent represents a rebate of your National Insurance and 3.8 per cent represents your employer's National Insurance.

If you newly contract out of SERPS before 5 April 1993, you (or your scheme) qualify for a special **incentive** payment equal to an extra two per cent a year of earnings between the upper and lower earnings limits. You'll usually count as 'newly' contracted out as long as:

- if you're contracted out through an employer's scheme, your job (rather than you personally) has not been contracted-out either through a current employer's pension scheme, or another scheme run by the same employer, since 1 January 1986
- if you're contracting out through a personal pension plan, you haven't voluntarily left an employer's contracted-out scheme since 6 April 1988, after being in the scheme for two years or more.

The incentive payment won't be payable for any years after 6 April 1993.

Table 24 on p. 107 gives a guide to the amount in £££ of rebate that would be paid into your contracted-out employer's money purchase scheme, or your contracted-out personal plan, depending on how much you earn. Obviously, the more that is invested in your contracted-out scheme or plan, the larger the amount of the eventual fund available to provide your pension. If you qualify for the incentive payment, contracting out will be more attractive than if you don't; and, if the rebate is revised downwards in 1993, contracting out will be more attractive now than later on.

The factors combined

Combining the four factors tells you that if you are male, young, and optimistic about future investment growth, contracting-out is likely to be a good move. If you're female, no longer so young and a pessimist, you'd be better off staying in SERPS. It's possible to be a little more precise than this by making an assumption about future investment performance. Table 23 overleaf provides a guide to whether contracting-out is likely to be worthwhile, assuming that investments grow at a 'middling' rate – neither very optimistic nor very pessimistic bearing in mind past long-term pension fund performance – and given the current size of rebate and incentive. There are still considerable grey areas, where there's no clear-cut guidance. If you fall into one of these areas, it would be a good idea to seek professional advice (see p. 108).

Table 23 is valid only while the rebate is at its present level. After 5 April 1993, the position will change. Your position will also change if you cross from one age band into another, or if your views on investment growth alter, so you should review periodically your contracting-out decision, unless you're already at an age where staying in SERPS is clearly your best option.

At present, you can contract out now, but contract back into SERPS at a later date. So there's nothing to stop you taking advantage of a contracted-out scheme or plan now, but rejoining SERPS when, for example, you get to the age at which SERPS benefits look more advantageous. There's always a risk that the government might close this option and make the contracting out decision a once-and-for-all choice – though this would be difficult for the government to implement, so the risk is probably slight.

Table 23: Should you consider contracting out?

Your age	If you qualify for the 2% incentive	If you don't qualify for the 2% incentive
WOMEN		
under 25	YES	YES
25 to 35	YES	MAYBE
35 to 40	MAYBE	NO
over 40	NO	NO
MEN		
under 35	YES	YES
35 to 45	YES	MAYBE
45 to 50	MAYBE	NO
over 50	NO	NO

A note of caution

According to the National Association of Pension Funds (NAPF) Survey, over 80 per cent of the employers' schemes surveyed are contracted out of SERPS. If you belong to a large final pay scheme, you're particularly likely to be contracted out through the scheme. Bear in mind that you can't lose by contracting out on a final pay basis – there's no need for you to consider contracting back in.

If you're contracted out through an employer's money purchase scheme (a COMP scheme) but find yourself in the group which would probably be better off contracted into SERPS, you should think carefully before making any decision. You can contract back in only by leaving the employer's scheme. But the scheme may be providing more generous benefits than just those required by the contracting-out rules. Leaving the scheme might mean you give up more than you gain by contracting back into SERPS. If in doubt, talk to the scheme officials (see p. 74) and consider getting independent advice (see p. 108).

Tax relief on your rebate

Employers' pension schemes

Contracting-out through an employer's pension scheme doesn't normally affect your income tax position: you pay less in National Insurance, but the earnings used as a basis for working out income tax are unchanged. If, however, your employer requires you to contribute to the pension scheme part of what you have saved by having to pay less National Insurance, the amount you contribute will be treated as a normal pension contribution for tax purposes. This means that the amount will be deducted from your pay before income tax is worked out, so you automatically get tax relief on the contribution at your highest rate (or rates) of tax.

Personal pension plans

Special tax rules apply to the rebate paid into a personal pension plan. You are given tax relief on the part of the rebate which represents your own National Insurance (in other words, two per cent of earnings between the upper and lower earnings limits given the present level of rebate). Tax relief is given only at the basic rate – even if you're a higher rate taxpayer. You don't receive the tax relief directly; instead, it's paid by the DSS into your personal pension plan along with the rebate. The tax relief represents, roughly, another 0.67 per cent of your earnings between the upper and lower earnings limits. There's no tax relief on any incentive payment, and there's no relief on the part of the rebate which represents National Insurance paid by your employer.

EXAMPLE

Ryan, who is 45 and a higher-rate taxpayer earning considerably more than the upper earnings limit for National Insurance, saves for retirement through a personal pension plan (see p. 84) and also has a separate appropriate personal pension to contract him out of SERPS. Ryan pays nothing directly to the appropriate plan but, after the end of each tax year, the Department of Social Security (DSS) paid an amount into it. For the 1989–90 tax year, the DSS paid in £1,242. This is made up of the following sums:

Rebate of Ryan's National Insurance	£	293
Rebate of his employer's National Insurance	£	558
2% incentive payment	£	293
Basic rate tax relief on rebate of Ryan's		
National Insurance	£	98
TOTAL	£1,242	

Free-standing AVC schemes

There's no tax relief on any part of the rebate paid into a free-standing AVC scheme, whereas you do get some tax relief when you contract out through a personal pension plan (see above). Since, in other respects, a contracted-out free-standing AVC scheme is virtually identical to a contracted-out personal pension plan, there's usually no advantage in choosing the free-standing AVC route. However, if you're already contributing to a free-standing AVC scheme, contracting out through it may be convenient for you, and you might save in plan charges (see p. 155) compared with contracting out through a separate personal pension plan.

How much is paid into your scheme or plan?

If you're contracted out through an employer's final pay scheme, your employer must make sure that enough is paid into the scheme eventually to provide at least the guaranteed amount of pension. Usually, any contribution you pay will be a set proportion (or set amount) of your salary. The employer will vary his contribution as necessary to ensure that the total being paid into the scheme is sufficient.

Table 24: What the government pays towards your contracted-out money purchase pension in the 1990–91 tax year [1]

Yearly earnings	Payment to an employer's money purchase scheme [2]		Payment to a contracted-out personal pension plan [3]	
	With 2% incentive £	*Without 2% incentive* £	*With 2% incentive* £	*Without 2% incentive* £
under £2,392 [4]	0	0	0	0
£ 5,000	203	151	220	168
£10,000	593	441	644	492
£11,000	671	499	728	556
£12,000	749	557	813	621
£13,000	827	615	898	686
£14,000	905	673	982	750
£15,000	983	731	1,067	815
£16,000	1,061	789	1,152	880
£17,000	1,139	847	1,236	944
£18,200 or more [5]	1,233	917	1,338	1,022

[1] Rounded to the nearest £

[2] Based on a rebate of 5.8% of earnings between lower and upper limits. Tax relief, if any, is paid to you, not into the scheme

[3] Based on a rebate of 5.8% of earnings between lower and upper earnings limits plus tax relief equal to a further 0.67%. Basic rate of tax was 25 per cent

[4] This is the lower earnings limit for the 1990–91 tax year

[5] This is the upper earnings limit for the 1990–91 tax year

The position with an employer's contracted-out money purchase scheme, or a personal pension plan, is rather different. The amount of the eventual pension is not guaranteed; instead, a minimum amount must be invested. The minimum must equal the rebate plus any incentive plus, in the case of personal plans, the tax relief provided by the government. Table 24 on p. 107 shows these minimum amounts for the 1990–91 tax year, depending on the level of your earnings.

More information

You may be in one of the groups for whom the decision about whether to be contracted in or contracted out of SERPS is reasonably clear, or you may be contracted out on a final pay basis in which case you do not need to take any action. But, if you're in that grey area where it's not clear whether contracting out is worthwhile for you, you'll need some help in making your decision.

A personal pension plan provider will give you an illustration of the possible pension from an appropriate personal pension (based on standard assumptions which they are legally obliged to use). Most providers will include with the illustration an estimate of the SERPS pension you would be giving up by contracting out. Bear in mind that illustrations give you *informed guesses* – it's impossible to know what the future benefits from a plan or from SERPS will be. See Chapter 12 for more details about personal plan illustrations.

If you belong to, or could join, an employer's pension scheme, you could ask the pension scheme administrators or trustees (see p. 74) to advise you – and they may be able to call on the services of a pensions consultant.

In an ideal world, it would also be sensible to get some completely independent advice. Independent advice about contracting out, and about any other aspect of your pension choices, is available from actuaries and from expert pensions consultants, but it's usually fairly expensive. Normally, you'll pay a fee based on the time spent on your case. You should establish the likely cost of the advice before going ahead. If independent advice is too costly for you alone, could you perhaps join forces with colleagues in a similar position and spread the cost between you? You can obtain a list of members of the following professional bodies, who provide independent advice, from the Society of Pension Consultants and the Association of Consulting Actuaries (addresses on pp. 215 and 213).

=8=

LEAVING A PENSION ARRANGEMENT BEFORE RETIREMENT

A great advantage of a personal pension plan is that it is personal to *you* and can be quite independent of *your job*. But employers' schemes are inevitably linked to your work, and changing jobs will affect your pension planning. Your employer's pension will be similarly affected, if you decide to opt out of the employer's scheme, even though you're not leaving the job.

If you have a personal plan, beware of switching to another, or of stopping a regular payment plan – there may be heavy penalties which severely reduce the amount of your savings.

Your right to a pension from an employer's scheme

If you leave an employer's pension scheme and you've been a member of it for two years or more, the scheme *must* either provide you with a pension at retirement – called a **preserved** or **deferred pension** – or allow you to transfer your pension rights to another pension scheme or plan.

Taking a refund

If you leave a scheme that you've belonged to for less than two years, you're not automatically entitled to any pension rights at all. More likely, you'll get a refund of your contributions. You can have back only contributions which you paid *yourself* – you can't have the amount of any contributions paid on your behalf by your employer. The trustees of the scheme have to hand over to the Inland Revenue tax on your refund, and usually the amount of the tax will be deducted from what you get. From the 1988–89 tax year onwards, the tax is paid at a special rate of 20 per cent (10 per cent in earlier years). If you're a non-taxpayer, you can't reclaim the tax; on the other hand, if you *are* a taxpayer, there's no more tax to pay.

There will also be a deduction – usually quite large – if you had been contracted out of SERPS through the employer's scheme. The scheme will arrange to 'buy you back' into the state scheme for the period you had been contracted out. The scheme has to pay over a sum of money – called the **contributions equivalent premium** – to the state, and part of this amount will be subtracted from your refund. The deduction is made before tax on the refund is worked out.

Your refund might include interest on your contributions – an annual survey of its members by the National Association of Pension Funds (NAPF) found that just over one-third of the schemes surveyed added interest to the repayment, though often at a very modest rate. If your scheme usually adds interest and at a reasonable rate, this can make the scheme a good place even for short-term investment: if you're a tax-payer, you'll have had tax relief at your full rate on the money you invested (your contributions) and your return is taxed at only 20 per cent – less than your normal rate.

If you've had a refund relating to a period that you'd been in an employer's scheme, the Inland Revenue deems that your earnings for that period are no longer covered by any pension arrangement. You can, instead, take out a personal pension plan to cover the period using the **carry forward rules** (see p. 88), as long as you do so within the time limits those rules allow. The tax rules let you have a refund of contributions that you made before 6 April 1975 regardless of how long you've been a member of your employer's pension scheme, but this is unlikley to be a wise move in view of the pension rights you'd lose.

Leaving an employer's final pay pension scheme

If you've been in an employer's final pay scheme (see p. 59) for two years or more, on leaving, the scheme must provide you with a preserved pension, or let you transfer your pension rights to another pension scheme or plan.

In a final pay scheme, your pension is worked out according to a formula, and is based on your years in the scheme (or working for the employer) and your pay. If you stay until retirement, your pay at that time is used in the calculation. But, if you leave before retirement, it's your pay at the time you leave that is relevant. Even ignoring inflation, in most cases, your pay as an 'early leaver' will be less than your pay at retirement would have been, because you'd normally expect pay increases due, for example, to promotion. This is one reason why changing jobs can lose you pension.

EXAMPLE

Megan, who works for a bank, has been a member of its pension scheme for four years. This is a final pay scheme which bases pensions on one-sixtieth of final pay for each year in the scheme. Megan earns £16,200 a year at present. With promotion, she could expect to earn at least £60,000 a year, in terms of today's money, by the time she reaches retirement. If her final pay at retirement were £60,000 a year, her four years to date in the scheme would be worth a pension of $4 \times \frac{1}{60} \times £60,000 = £4,000$ a year in today's money. But Megan is thinking about leaving the bank and taking a job that follows her interest in art instead. If she leaves the bank's pension scheme now, her four years will have earned her a preserved pension of only $4 \times \frac{1}{60} \times £16,200 = £1,080$ a year. The preserved pension must be increased to at least partially protect it against inflation (see opposite). Whether Megan gains or loses pension because of her job move depends on many factors, including inflation, her prospects in her new job, her new pension arrangements, and so on.

The effect of inflation

There is a second way in which you may lose pension, if you leave a final pay scheme before retirement. If you've left an employer's pension scheme before 1 January 1986, the scheme is under no obligation at all to increase your preserved pension (other than contracted-out pension rights – see below) between the time you left and the time when it will eventually be paid to you. Inflation severely eats into the buying power of these unprotected preserved pensions.

For people leaving an employer's scheme on or after 1 January 1986, pension rights built up from 1 January 1985 onwards must be at least partly protected against inflation. This is done by requiring the scheme to increase the preserved pension in line with inflation, or by five per cent a year if this is lower (but see p. 114 for the rules concerning contracted-out pension rights). Your preserved pension is still at the mercy of inflation, if prices rise on average by more than five per cent a year, and if you built up pension rights before 1985. Historically, earnings have tended to rise faster than prices, so the link to price inflation may still mean that your pension lags behind.

At the time of writing, the government has proposed a change in the law to require employer's schemes to protect *all* pension rights – including pre-1985 rights – against inflation up to a maximum of five per cent a year. Good schemes already tend to do this, and may be prepared to increase preserved pensions by more if inflation is higher – though such increases are rarely, if ever, guaranteed.

Contracted-out pension rights

If you're contracted out through a final pay scheme which you then leave, the scheme is obliged to protect your contracted-out pension rights – in other words, your guaranteed minimum pension (GMP) and widow's or widower's GMP. The amount of GMP you're entitled to at the time you leave is calculated. It must then be increased until the time at which you reach the state pension age. The scheme can choose one of three ways in which to make the increases:

- in line with increases in national average earnings
- by a fixed amount of 7.5 per cent a year (8.5 per cent for people who left a scheme before 6 April 1988)
- in line with earnings inflation up to a maximum of 5 per cent, as long as the scheme makes a payment to the State called a **limited revaluation premium**.

If, with the last two methods, the revalued GMPs fall short of GMPs increased in line with average earnings in the nation as a whole, the State makes good the shortfall.

GMPs can be transferred to another pension scheme or plan, as long as that scheme or plan can be used for contracted-out pension rights (see p. 120).

Leaving an employer's money purchase scheme

If, on changing jobs, you leave an employer's money purchase scheme after two years' membership or more, you stop contributing to the scheme, and your employer stops making contributions on your behalf. But the money already invested continues to grow as before, and you'll get the full benefit of the fund which has built up by the time you retire. Alternatively, you can transfer the fund which has built up to another pension scheme or plan.

The amount in a money purchase preserved fund is quite independent of your level of pay on leaving, and doesn't suffer from the potential drawbacks of a final pay preserved pension (see p. 112). In general, you can't lose pension, if you're an early leaver from a money purchase scheme.

Changing jobs if you have a personal plan

If you have a single lump sum contribution personal pension plan, changing jobs has no affect at all on the plan. And, if you have a regular contribution personal plan, you can usually keep your plan going without any alteration, if you change jobs. There are three exceptions:

- if you have a contracted-out personal plan (see Chapter 7) for which you cease to be eligible. This would happen if you switched from being an employee to self-employed status instead. It would also happen if you decided to join a new employer's scheme which was itself a contracted-out scheme. In both cases, you would not be able to continue claiming the National Insurance rebate for your personal plan
- if you have a (non-contracted-out) personal plan for which you cease to be eligible. This would happen, if your new employer runs a pension scheme which you decide to join. You can't simultaneously belong to an employer's scheme and have a personal plan (except where the employer's scheme is a contracted-in one, and you're using a personal plan solely for contracting out)
- if your old employer had been paying some or all of the contributions to your personal plan. You'll need to investigate whether you can keep the plan going with lower contributions, with contributions from your new employer, or by paying in more yourself.

If you do have to stop paying into your personal plan, you can't get back any money already paid into it, except as a pension (and any tax-free lump sum for which you're eligible at your pension age). And, to do this, you must have reached the earliest pension age recognised by the tax rules and the plan provider.

If you stop paying into a regular payment personal plan, usually your fund continues to be invested, and it carries on growing as before to provide your eventual pension and any other benefits. Alternatively, you can transfer the fund to another pension plan or scheme – for example, you might want to invest it in your new employer's scheme. Likewise, you can transfer the fund built up in a single contribution personal plan, if you wish.

If you have to stop paying into a regular contribution plan, the eventual pension will of course be smaller than originally expected, because you'll have put less money into the plan. However, if you stop paying in the early years, the most severe effect will be due to charges. There are a variety of charges (and/or expenses) to be met out of your contributions (see p. 155). These give the plan provider its profit margin, and cover its costs which are usually particularly heavy when the plan is first set up (see p. 172). If you keep up the plan as originally intended, the charges are effectively spread over a long period of time and have a proportionately small impact on your overall return. But, if you stop the plan in the early years, a large chunk of the charges will usually be set against your fund – which is as yet relatively small. This can drastically reduce the amount in your plan and, in some cases, can reduce your fund to nothing. This means your plan has a low value – or, at worst, no value at all – whether you leave it invested or transfer to another plan or scheme.

With some personal plans, you may be able to stop your regular payments and leave the fund invested, but then restart your contributions at a later date if your circumstances change again – this will help to absorb the impact of charges. Whether or not this is possible, and the terms which apply, depend on the rules of the particular plan.

Transferring your pension rights

Since 1 January 1986, anyone leaving an employer's pension scheme who has a right to a preserved pension, also has the right to take a **transfer value** instead. A transfer value is a lump sum which is judged to be equivalent to the preserved pension (and any other rights) given up. You can't receive the transfer value as cash in hand, though – it must be reinvested in another pension scheme or plan.

Both old- and new-style personal pension plans must also give you the right to a transfer value, if you wish to switch the fund you have built up to another pension arrangement.

There are a variety of ways in which you can reinvest a transfer value – they are summarised in Table 25 below. But note that, while all employers' schemes and personal pension plans must give you the right to *take* a transfer value, there is no obligation on any scheme or plan to *accept* your transfer value.

Table 25: Transferring your pension savings

Your current method of pension saving	Your transfer choices
Old-style personal plan	New-style personal plan *or* employer's scheme
New-style personal plan – not contracted out	Another new-style plan *or* employer's scheme
New-style personal plan – contracted out	Another contracted-out new-style personal plan *or* contracted-out employer's scheme
Employer's scheme – not contracted out	Another employer's scheme *or* new-style personal plan *or* section 32 plan (see p. 120)
Employer's scheme – contracted out	Another contracted-out employer's scheme *or* contracted-in employer's scheme and bought back into SERPS *or* contracted-out new-style personal plan *or* section 32 plan (see p. 120)

How much is the transfer value?

If you are switching your pension rights from an employer's money purchase scheme, or a personal pension plan (which also works on the money purchase basis), the transfer value is simply the value of your fund – in other words, the contributions plus their investment growth less any deductions for charges and expenses.

If you are switching from a final pay scheme, the transfer value must be worked out by the scheme's actuary. He makes assumptions, for example about future investment growth, and works back to arrive at a lump sum which, if invested now, could reasonably be expected to produce enough to pay the amount of your preserved pension at retirement (together with any other rights, such as widow's or widower's pensions, guaranteed pension increases, and so on). The figure for the lump sum is the amount of your transfer value.

As the transfer value is the cash equivalent of your pension rights, a transfer value relating to a final pay scheme incorporates any 'loss' you might be making as a result of leaving the scheme.

What will the transfer value buy?

If you're transferring into a money purchase pension scheme or plan, the transfer value will simply be added to your fund and invested until it is used to provide your retirement pension or other benefits.

If you're transferring into a final pay scheme, the transfer value might be used in a number of ways, for example:

- it could be used now to 'buy' a fixed amount of pension at retirement
- it could be used now to buy 'extra years' in the scheme, so that you're credited with more years of membership than you will have in reality. Via the pension formula, these years are translated into a higher pension and other benefits
- it could be invested as a separate fund to be used at retirement to 'buy' extra benefits in the main scheme – in a similar way to an AVC scheme.

Buying extra years, in particular, often causes some confusion, because the number of years credited in the new scheme is invariably less than the number of years you had belonged to the old scheme. But it's easy to see why the difference arises: the transfer value from the old scheme reflects your preserved pension. In the case of a final pay scheme, this was based on your pay when you left the scheme and the amount by which the preserved pension will be increased up to retirement. In the new scheme, your transfer value is used to 'buy' an equivalent amount of pension but, this time, it will be based on your pay at retirement. Since this is generally expected to be higher than your pay on leaving the old scheme, the transfer value equates to fewer years in the new scheme than in the old.

EXAMPLE

Megan decides to leave the bank for which she works. After a year of trying to get a job in the art world, she decides to return to banking and joins a large merchant banking conglomerate. Her new employer runs a final pay pension scheme, which will accept a transfer value from Megan's old employer's scheme. For simplicity, this example ignores the increases which must by law be made to Megan's preserved pension, so we'll assume that her four years in the old pension scheme are worth a preserved pension of £1,080 a year (in today's money). The actuary of the old scheme calculates that a lump sum of £5,600 would, if invested now, be enough to provide that pension. In the new scheme, it's estimated that her pay at retirement might be £65,000 (in today's money). Thus, each year in the new scheme would provide her with $\frac{1}{60} \times £65,000 = £1,083$. The actuary of the new scheme works out that the transfer value is, on his assumptions about future investment performance and earnings growth, enough to buy about one year's worth of future pension. So Megan gives up four years of membership in her old scheme for just one year in the new scheme, but the preserved pension of £1,080 a year she gives up is virtually identical to the £1,083 a year pension she is expected to get from the new scheme as a result of the one year with which she's credited.

Transferring contracted-out pension rights

The guarantees associated with contracting out must continue even if the benefits are transferred. This is the case whether you're contracted out through a final pay scheme which provides a guaranteed minimum pension (GMP), or through a money purchase arrangement which merely guarantees that minimum contributions will be used to provide the protected rights (see Chapter 7).

If you're contracted-out, you can transfer your contracted-out pension rights to a new employer's contracted-out scheme, to a section 32 plan (see below), or to an appropriate personal pension plan. If you transfer from a contracted-out final pay scheme to a money purchase scheme or plan, you'll lose the right to a GMP – instead you'll get money purchase contracted-out rights. In other words, the transfer value of the GMP will have to be invested to provide the protected rights pensions – a retirement pension and a widow's or widower's pension.

If you transfer the rest of your pension rights to a new employer's scheme which is contracted in and thus can't accept contracted-out rights, your old scheme can either continue to preserve just your GMP, or it can arrange for you to be 'bought back' into the state scheme by paying a **transfer premium** to the state. If you're 'bought back' in this way, you'll no longer get a GMP at retirement from the old employer's scheme; instead, you'll get SERPS pension from the state.

Transferring to a section 32 plan

Section 32 plans – also called **buy-out bonds** – are a special type of personal pension plan designed to accept transfer values from employers' pension schemes. The transfer value is paid into the plan and invested on a money purchase basis. The fund which builds up is then used to provide a retirement pension and any other benefits. Section 32 plans were first introduced in 1981; since July 1988 new-style personal pension plans have provided an alternative to them.

Section 32 plans can be used to preserve contracted-out pension rights, and can be a good idea in the case of transfers from contracted-out final pay schemes. The section 32 plan must take over the guarantee to provide a set amount of GMP at retirement. To do this, the plan provider needs to be satisfied that the transfer value is sufficient. By contrast, if you transfer from a contracted-out final pay scheme to a contracted-out new-style personal plan, you give up your right to a guaranteed amount of pension, though you get protected rights instead. With a personal plan, you take the risk that the transfer value might provide a smaller pension than the GMP you gave up; with a section 32 plan, the plan provider takes that risk.

Winding up

Until now, if your employer's scheme is wound up (for example, in the event of your employer going bust, or being taken over by another firm which doesn't wish to continue the scheme), protection for your pension rights has been fairly limited: you have been *entitled* only to the benefits that an early leaver could get. In practice, you might get more generous benefits, but that has been dependent on the generosity of the scheme rather than your rights in law.

At the time of writing, the government has proposed new legislation to improve the benefits that **must** be provided for members in the event of a scheme being wound up. Provided the scheme is wound up after the new law comes into force, the whole of your preserved pension (not just the part which has built up since 1 January 1985) must be increased in line with inflation up to a maximum of five per cent a year up to the time you retire. Also, the pension must be increased in line with inflation to a maximum of five per cent a year once it starts to be paid. The proposed legislation will introduce other protective measures, including a requirement that at least one of the trustees of a scheme must be an independent person in a case where the employer has gone bust.

=9=

HELP IN THE EVENT OF DEATH

Pension schemes don't just provide you with an income in old age. They can also be used to provide financial support for your widow, widower, children and other dependants in the event of your death. Sometimes these benefits form an automatic part of the pension scheme or plan; sometimes they are optional extras.

What the state provides for widows

What help your widow could get from the state in the event of your death depends on the record of National Insurance you'd built up. Assuming you'd paid enough contributions – see Chart 10 overleaf – she could be entitled to some or all of the following state benefits:

- **widow's payment**   This is a lump sum of £1,000
- **widowed mother's allowance**   This is a regular income that your widow can get if she is caring for your children
- **widow's pension**   This is a regular income for widows aged 45 or more who haven't any dependent children.

Chart 10 summarises the state help available for widows.

The amount of the widow's payment has not changed since it was introduced in April 1988, but the widowed mother's allowance and widow's pension are both increased each year in line with changes in the Retail Prices Index – in common with other state pensions. There's no tax to pay on

Chart 10: Help from the state for widows and widowers

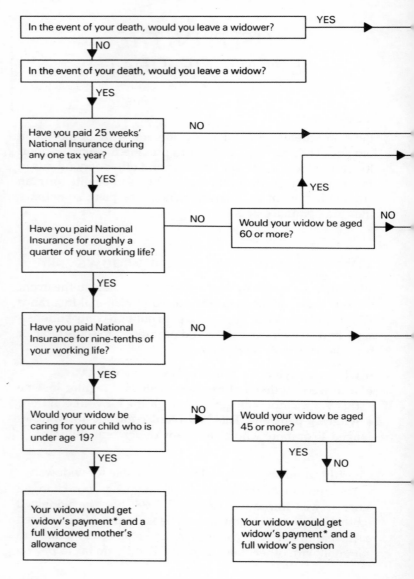

In the event of your death, would you leave a widower? — YES →

NO ↓

In the event of your death, would you leave a widow?

YES ↓

Have you paid 25 weeks' National Insurance during any one tax year? — NO →

YES ↓

Have you paid National Insurance for roughly a quarter of your working life? — NO → Would your widow be aged 60 or more? — NO → / YES ↑

YES ↓

Have you paid National Insurance for nine-tenths of your working life? — NO →

YES ↓

Would your widow be caring for your child who is under age 19? — NO → Would your widow be aged 45 or more? — YES ↓ / NO ↓

YES ↓

Your widow would get widow's payment* and a full widowed mother's allowance

Your widow would get widow's payment* and a full widow's pension

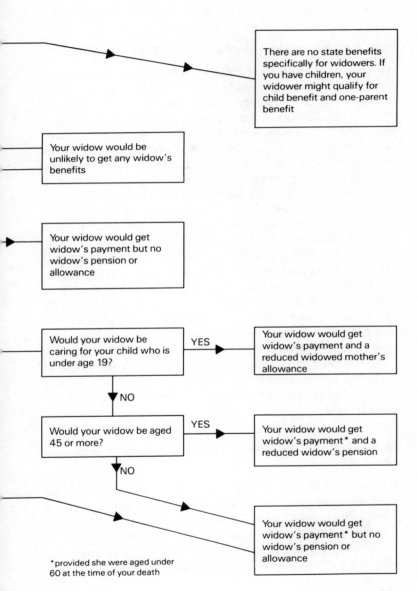

There are no state benefits specifically for widowers. If you have children, your widower might qualify for child benefit and one-parent benefit

Your widow would be unlikely to get any widow's benefits

Your widow would get widow's payment but no widow's pension or allowance

Would your widow be caring for your child who is under age 19?

YES

Your widow would get widow's payment and a reduced widowed mother's allowance

NO

Would your widow be aged 45 or more?

YES

Your widow would get widow's payment* and a reduced widow's pension

NO

Your widow would get widow's payment* but no widow's pension or allowance

*provided she were aged under 60 at the time of your death

125

the widow's payment, but widowed mother's allowance and widow's pension both count as income for tax purposes.

Help for your widow if you have dependent children

Whether or not you have children, your widow can receive the widow's payment provided she is under 60 and you were not receiving (or eligible for) a basic state retirement pension. She will be eligible for the widowed mother's allowance, if you have a **dependent** child or children. A child is dependent, if your widow can claim child benefit (see below) for him or her – this will be the case for most children up to the age of 18. Your widow usually continues to get the allowance for as long as she is caring for the children. But the allowance stops if she remarries. When the youngest child no longer counts as dependent, your widow may be able to get a widow's pension (see below) instead.

In the 1990–91 tax year, the widowed mother's allowance is £46.90 a week plus £9.65 a week for each child. On top of this, your widow receives any State Earnings Related Pension Scheme (SERPS) pension that you've built up (see Chapter 4). The SERPS pension is reduced, if she can get a contracted-out widow's pension from your employer's pension scheme (see p. 132) or your personal pension plan (see p. 137).

Your widow will normally carry on getting **child benefit** for each of your children under the age of 19. This is £7.25 a week for each child in the 1990–91 tax year. There's no tax to pay on child benefit.

Help for your widow if you don't have dependent children

If your widow is aged less than 60, and you were not receiving (or entitled to) a basic state retirement pension, she can qualify for the lump sum widow's payment.

If you have no children, or they are all over the age of 18, your widow can't qualify for anything more than the widow's payment unless she is at least 45.

Widows aged 45 or over, without dependent children, can get a widow's pension. This applies to women who are that age when first widowed. It also applies to women who are that age when their youngest, or only, child ceases to be dependent, and thus they cease to qualify for the widowed mother's allowance. Usually, the pension continues to be paid until your widow qualifies for a state retirement pension. But, if she remarries, the widow's pension stops.

The amount of widow's pension varies according to the woman's age at the time she was first widowed. The highest rate is payable to widows who were aged 55 or over. If the woman was younger than this, the lower rate continues to apply year after year. The different rates of widow's pension are shown in Table 26 below.

Table 26: Amount of widow's pension in the 1990–91 tax year

Age of widow at the time of husband's death [1]	Amount of widow's pension £££ per week
45	14.07
46	17.35
47	20.64
48	23.92
49	27.20
50	30.49
51	33.77
52	37.05
53	40.33
54	43.62
55 or over	46.90

[1] For women widowed before 6 April 1988, the relevant ages are five years younger, with the full rate pension payable for new widows aged 50 or over

Your widow may also be entitled to any SERPS pension you'd built up. The full amount of SERPS pension is payable to widow's aged 55 or over. But women who were younger than this when first widowed receive a reduced amount of SERPS pension.

Switching to retirement pension

A widow who is receiving widowed mother's allowance or widow's pension at the time she reaches the normal state pension age of 60 has a choice:

- she can give up the allowance or widow's pension and receive retirement pension instead. The retirement pension will be at least as big as the allowance or widow's pension given up. On top of that, your widow will also receive any SERPS pension she qualifies for in her own right, plus her own graduated pension (if any) and half of your graduated pension (if any)
- she can continue to receive the widowed mother's allowance (as long as she continues to qualify for it) or widow's pension. But at age 65, she will have to switch to retirement pension
- she can give up the widowed mother's allowance or widow's pension *and* not start to receive retirement pension, in order to earn extra pension. This works in the same way as earning extra pension by deferring your retirement pension (see p. 33).

The retirement pension your widow receives may be a pension based on her own National Insurance record, or a mixture of her own and your National Insurance.

What if you hadn't paid enough National Insurance?

Widow's payment is payable at just one rate: if you'd paid enough National Insurance, your widow receives the full amount; if you hadn't paid enough National Insurance, she gets nothing.

Widowed mother's allowance and widow's pension are based on the National Insurance you'd paid during your working life (see p. 37). If you hadn't paid enough for your widow to receive the full rate of allowance or pension, she may instead receive a reduced-rate allowance or pension. She should get at least some pension or allowance as long as you've paid National Insurance for a quarter of your working life.

What the state provides for widowers

There are no formal state benefits for widowers and, if you have no dependent children, your widower will usually get no help at all from the state. If you have children under the age of 19, your widower can claim child benefit (see p. 126) and he may also qualify for **one parent benefit**. This is available to single parents bringing up one or more children on their own. The child must live with the parent – not just be supported by him. The benefit is usually payable as long as the parent is entitled to claim child benefit, but payment will stop if your widower remarries (or cohabits as if he were married).

In the 1990–91 tax year, one parent benefit is paid at a single rate of £5.60 a week (even if you have more than one child). It is usually increased each year in line with the Retail Prices Index. There's no income tax to pay on one parent benefit. Chart 10 on pp. 124 and 125 summarises the help available from the state for widowers.

Other help from the state

Widows and widowers on low incomes may qualify for **non-contributory benefits**, such as **income support** and **housing benefit**. These benefits are not covered in this book. You can find out about them by contacting your local Department of Social Security (see p. 35).

Help from your employer before retirement

If you belong to an employer's pension scheme, your dependants will almost certainly be entitled to benefits which are payable in the event of your death before retirement. These will usually take the form of:

- lump sum life insurance
- often a refund of your contributions to the pension scheme
- a pension for your widow or widower
- and possibly pensions for your children or other dependants.

Some employers have schemes to provide some or all of these benefits even for employees who are not covered by a pension scheme run by the employer.

How much as a lump sum?

The taxman gives tax relief on the amount of money paid in and invested to provide life cover, so naturally enough the taxman also sets limits on the amount of cover which can be provided in this way.

The general rule is that the maximum lump sum which can be paid out in the event of death must not be greater than four times the employee's **final pay**, which is broadly pay just before, or near, the time of death. For schemes set up on or after 14 March 1989, or for employees joining a scheme on or after 1 June 1989, there is also an overall cash limit on the amount of life cover. In the 1990–91 tax year, this limit is £259,200. This cash limit will increase each year in line with the Retail Prices Index. Life insurance payable from previous pension schemes and plans that you had counts towards the Inland Revenue maximum.

The tax rules also allow the amount of your (but not your employer's) contributions to the pension scheme to be paid out as a lump sum, in addition to the main amount of cover described above. In some cases, interest is added to the repayment of contributions.

The employer's scheme can also set its own limit which may be lower than those set by the Inland Revenue. For example, the National Association of Pension Funds (NAPF) survey of its members found that about a quarter of the pension schemes covered have life cover of less than three times salary.

In most schemes, the scheme has the right to decide who will receive the lump sum in the event of your death. (This prevents the lump sum being counted as part of your estate for inheritance tax purposes.) In practice, the scheme will usually pay the money to whomever you have requested – though it would probably override your wishes if you'd failed to name someone who could prove to have been genuinely dependent on you. You should review your request whenever your circumstances change – say, on marriage, or the birth of a child.

How much widow's or widower's pension?

The taxman also limits the amount that can be paid out in pensions to a widow or widower and other dependants. The general rule is that a widow's or widower's pension must not be greater than two-thirds of the *maximum* pension that the employee could have had. 'Maximum' means the maximum according to the tax rules – in other words, based on the taxman's definition of final pay and the number of years that the employee could have been in the scheme (or in that particular employment) had he remained in the scheme until normal retirement. For schemes set up on or after 14 March 1989, or for employees joining a scheme on or after 1 June 1989, there is also an overall cash limit on the widow's or widower's pension. The limit is two-thirds of £43,200 for the 1990–91 tax year; the limit will increase each year in line with the Retail Prices Index. Table 27 overleaf gives a guide to the maximum pension your widow or widower could receive depending on your pay.

Table 27: The maximum widow's or widower's pension from an employer's scheme [1]

Your earnings from the employer	Maximum widow's or widower's pension
£££ per year	£££ per year
10,000	4,444
15,000	6,667
20,000	8,889
25,000	11,111
30,000	13,333
40,000	17,778
50,000	22,222
60,000	26,667
70,000	31,111 [2]
80,000	35,556 [2]

[1] If you joined the pension scheme on or after 17 March 1987, you must have worked for the employer for 20 years up to the time of death for the maximum widow's pension to be payable. If you joined before 17 March 1987, 10 years' service is sufficient

[2] Or £28,800 in the 1990–91 tax year for a scheme set up on or after 14 March 1989, or an employee joining a scheme on or after 1 June 1989

The Inland Revenue's limit applies to the sum of benefits from all schemes or plans to which you have belonged, or still belong. So widows' or widowers' pensions payable from schemes you had belonged to in the past must be taken into account when working out the most that your current scheme could pay.

Once the upper limit on the widow's or widower's pension has been found, it can be increased each year in line with the Retail Prices Index. This provides a ceiling within which the actual pension a scheme pays must remain. Most schemes increase widows' or widowers' pensions by less than the maximum that the tax rules allow.

If you were contracted-out through your employer's pension scheme and it was a final pay scheme, your widow's pension must include a guaranteed minimum pension (GMP) (see p. 94) of at least half the amount of GMP you had built up, provided your widow is 45 or over, or has dependent children. There are special rules concerning increases to GMPs once they have started to be paid (see p. 99).

If you were contracted out through an employer's money purchase scheme, the whole of your protected rights 'fund' must be converted into pension for your widow if you're a man, or widower if you're a woman.

A scheme can set its own limit on the pension it will pay provided it doesn't break the taxman's limit. Over three-quarters of the schemes covered by the NAPF survey provide widows' or widowers' pensions of only half the employee's pension entitlement, and only just over half of the schemes based the widow's or widower's pension on the pension the employee could have had *if he or she had been in the scheme until normal retirement*. Not so long ago, it was rare for an employer's pension scheme to provide *widowers'* pensions at all. But by 1988, only a tenth of the schemes in the NAPF survey provided no widower's pension at all, and nearly a half provided such a pension even if the widower had not been financially dependent on his wife.

The scheme rules will determine whether a widow's or widower's pension is payable for life – usually it is. About a quarter of the schemes in the NAPF survey either stop paying, or review the position, if the widow or widower remarries.

Pension for other dependants

In the event of your death before retirement, your employer's pension scheme can provide a pension for one or more dependants other than your widow or widower. Any one pension can't be more than two-thirds of the maximum retirement pension you could have had – this is the same as the limit applied to the widow's or widower's pension (see p. 131).

A pension for a dependent child must cease when the child stops being dependent – for example, when the child reaches age 19, or when he or she finishes their full-time education. Pensions for other dependants can continue for the rest of their lives, even if they cease to be dependent in the literal sense of the word.

All the dependants' pensions – whether for your widow or widower, a child or children or some other dependant, such as an elderly relative – when added together must not come to more than the maximum amount which could have been paid to you as retirement pension.

Help from your employer after retirement

An employer's pension scheme may also provide help for dependants in the event of your death after retirement. This can take a number of forms:

- a separate widow's or widower's pension
- pension for other dependants
- guaranteed payment of your own pension for a set number of years, if you die within that time
- possibly, a lump sum.

How much widow's or widower's pension?

As with pensions payable on death before retirement, the Inland Revenue limits the maximum pension that can be automatically provided for a widow or widower. The limit is two-thirds of the *maximum* retirement pension to which you could have been entitled. 'Maximum' relates to the taxman's definition of final pay, though the calculation is based on the *actual* number of years you had worked for your employer. Once it starts to be paid, the widow's or widower's pension can be increased as long as it does not exceed the maximum possible pension increased in line with changes in the Retail Prices Index.

If you're contracted-out of SERPS through a final pay scheme, the scheme must provide a widow's pension of at least half the GMP (see p. 94) that you have built up. Since 6 April 1988, there must also have been provision for a GMP to be paid to widowers, provided you were receiving a state basic pension and your husband is getting either a basic pension or a state invalidity pension. There are special rules concerning increases in GMPs once they start to be paid (see p. 99).

If you're contracted out through a money purchase scheme, the protected rights must include a widow's or widower's pension of half the amount you had been getting in protected rights retirement pension.

The scheme can set its own limit on the widow's or widower's pension, and one-half of the employee's retirement pension is most commonly used. In the majority of schemes, the widow's or widower's pension is based on the employee's potential retirement pension *before* any deduction is made to take account of the employee taking a tax-free lump sum (see p. 62).

According to the NAPF survey, most schemes pay the widow's or widower's pension for life, though about a fifth of the schemes surveyed either stopped the pension, or reviewed it, if the widow or widower remarried. The same survey found that about a quarter of the schemes let you increase the pension that your widow or widower would get by giving up part of your retirement pension – you make this decision at the time you retire. The total widow's pension (including any amount provided automatically under the scheme) must not come to more than your remaining retirement pension.

Pensions for other dependants

The scheme can provide pensions for other dependants, such as children or elderly relatives. No one pension can exceed two-thirds of the maximum retirement pension you could have had; and all dependants' pensions (including a widow's or widower's pension) must not, in total, come to more than the full amount of retirement pension you could have had.

Children's pensions are payable only until they cease to be dependent – for example, on reaching age 18 or ceasing full-time education. Other dependants' pensions can be payable for life.

Guaranteed payment of your own pension

An employer's pension scheme can guarantee to pay your retirement pension for up to 10 years, in case your death occurs before that time is up. Other rules make a 10-year guarantee impractical for most schemes. But a five-year guarantee is both practical and in use in many employer's schemes.

Usually, the scheme has the right to decide who should receive your pension if, after your death, it continues to be paid for the rest of a guarantee period. But, in practice, your request will usually be respected. Often, the guaranteed pension is 'rolled up' and paid immediately as a lump sum (see below). If your widow or widower is to receive periodic payments of the guaranteed pension, it will usually be paid alongside any dependant's pension he or she receives.

A lump sum

If you retire at the normal retirement date for your scheme, your employer normally won't provide you with life cover after retirement. However, if your death occurred relatively soon after retirement, the scheme might pay out a lump sum if the payment of your pension had been guaranteed (as described above), or if you'd received less in pension than the amount you'd contributed to the scheme over the years.

Help through a personal pension plan before retirement

A personal pension plan can be used to provide:

- a pension for your widow or widower

- a pension for your children or other dependants
- lump sum from your pension plan
- lump sum life cover through a related term insurance policy.

With the exception of contracted-out plans (see below), you can choose whether or not to include benefits to be paid in the event of death. The more benefits you decide to include, the less of your fund will be available to provide your retirement pension. But, if you have dependants, it's important that you make provision for them, and using a pension plan can be one of the most tax-efficient ways of doing this.

How much pension for your dependants?

A contracted-out personal plan (see Chapter 7) *must* allow for a widow's or widower's pension to be payable if your widow or widower is aged 45 or over, or if they are younger than 45 but qualify for child benefit – these conditions tie in with the widow's benefits available from the State (see p. 126). The pension would be whatever amount can be bought by the fund built up through investing the contracting-out rebates (together with tax relief and incentive payments, if applicable). Your widow or widower has an **open market option** which gives them the right to shop around for a different pension provider rather than stay with the original plan provider.

The pension *may* cease if your widow or widower remarries while under the state pension age, or ceases to be eligible for child benefit and is still under the age of 45 – but the pension provider can choose to carry on paying the pension in these circumstances.

A contracted-out widow's or widower's pension must be increased each year in line with inflation up to a maximum of three per cent a year.

If you have no widow or widower, the fund built up by the invested rebates can be paid to another dependant or, failing that, paid to your estate, or to someone you nominate.

With personal plans, other than contracted-out plans (or the contracted-out element of a plan), you can arrange for a pension to be paid to your widow, widower, children and/or other dependants in the event of death. With an old-style plan, the amount of money that has built up in your fund is the only limit on the size of the pension, or pensions, that can be paid. With a new-style plan, there is also a restriction that the total of pensions for dependants must not come to more than the amount of retirement pension which your fund could have bought if you could have retired at the time of death.

How much lump sum?

If your plan doesn't include any arrangements for paying pensions to dependants, or if you have no dependants, a lump sum can be paid from your plan. With an old-style scheme, this is the amount of your accumulated fund. With a new-style scheme, the lump sum is either the accumulated fund, or could be equal to the return of contributions together with reasonable interest and bonuses. The lump sum doesn't have to be paid to someone who was financially dependent on you.

How much life cover?

You can use up to five per cent of your **net relevant earnings** (see p. 84) in premiums for a special life insurance policy used to pay out a lump sum in the event of your death before 75. You get tax relief at your highest rate on the premiums, but the amount you pay counts towards your overall contribution limit for personal pension plans (see Chapter 6). This means that, if you want to pay the maximum possible towards your pension, you may do better to arrange separate life insurance outside your personal pension arrangement.

When connected to an old-style personal plan, the life insurance is called a **section 226A policy**. When connected to a new-style plan, it is called a **section 621 policy**. Basically these two policies are the same.

Help through a personal plan after retirement

With the exception of contracted-out plans, you must choose at the time you start to take your pension which death benefits you want to have as part of your plan. They might include:

- a guarantee that your pension will continue for a set period, in case death occurs within that time
- a pension for your widow or widower
- a pension for other dependants
- the equivalent of any guaranteed pension can be paid as a lump sum.

Pension guarantee

You can arrange for your retirement pension to carry on being paid for a set period after the date of your retirement, in case your death occurs within that time. The guarantee period can't be longer than ten years. You can nominate the person who will receive your pension if you die within the period – or the lump sum equivalent of it. The recipient doesn't have to be financially dependent on you.

How much pension for your dependants?

A contracted-out personal plan must allow for a widow's or widower's pension as described on p. 137. The sum of any pensions for your widow, widower and/or other dependants from a plan which is not contracted-out must not come to more than the amount of pension that you were receiving. Otherwise there is no limit on the amount of these pensions.

══ 10 ══

EARLY RETIREMENT

For many people, the idea of early retirement is attractive. But you'll usually have to rely on a smaller pension than you'd otherwise have had. You need to plan ahead if you're to be able to afford to give up work early. But, if ill health forces you to retire early, your pension may be protected to some extent – it all depends on the particular rules of your pension scheme or plan.

The state scheme

Choosing early retirement

You can't receive a state retirement pension earlier than the official pension age of 65 for men or 60 for women. Your plans for early retirement will need to take account of this: if you retire before state pension age, you may need income from another source to make up for the lack of state pension; once you are 65 (men) or 60 (women) your income may increase as your state pension starts.

You'll also need to consider whether to continue paying National Insurance after you retire – if you stop, your National Insurance record might not be sufficient for you to qualify for a full state basic pension (see Chapter 3).

Retiring due to ill health

Even if you have to give up work because of ill health or disability, you can't receive the state basic, or graduated, retirement pension early. However, you might qualify for some other help from the state.

If you're temporarily ill, you may qualify for **statutory sick pay** paid through your employer if you're an employee, or **state sickness benefit** if you're self-employed or not working. If you're still unwell after 28 weeks and you've paid the appropriate National Insurance while you were working, you'll be transferred to the longer-term state **invalidity benefit**. This can be made up of a number of parts:

- **invalidity pension**   This is the basic invalidity benefit. It's a weekly payment equal to the amount of the state basic retirement pension – £46.90 in the 1990–91 tax year. You get extra if you have dependants, such as a wife and children
- **additional invalidity pension**   This is an earnings-related addition to the basic invalidity pension. It's based on your earnings above the lower earnings limit on which you've paid Class 1 National Insurance (in a similar manner to your SERPS entitlement – see p. 47). The government is phasing out this part of invalidity benefit, and no *new* entitlements can be built up from 6 April 1991 onwards. Additional invalidity pension in respect of entitlement built up before that date will continue to be payable
- **invalidity allowance**   This is an extra payment that you can get if you were under the age of 60 (men) or 55 (women) when your illness started. There are three rates – which one you get depends on your age at the start of the illness (see Table 28 below).

Table 28: Rates of invalidity allowance in the 1990–91 tax year

Age at the start of your illness		Weekly allowance
Men	*Women*	£
Under 40	Under 40	10.00
40–49	40–49	6.20
50–59	50–54	3.10

141

Invalidity allowance is reduced by the amount of any additional invalidity pension that you get.

If your illness or disability continues until you reach state pension age, you'll usually stop getting invalidity benefit and receive your retirement pension instead. If you put off the start of your retirement pension, you can carry on getting invalidity benefit but the invalidity pension will be paid only at whatever rate of state basic pension you'd otherwise be getting; in other words, if you'd be getting a reduced rate basic pension, your invalidity pension will be reduced to that level once you reach state pension age. (But, if you're unable to work because of an industrial injury or an industrial disease, your invalidity benefit won't be reduced in this way.) At age 70 (men) or 65 (women), you have to switch to retirement pension.

If you're receiving invalidity benefit, deferring the start of your state retirement pension won't earn you extra pension. But, it will often be worthwhile delaying the switch to retirement pension because invalidity benefit is not taxable, whereas the retirement pension counts as income for tax purposes.

If you continue to receive additional invalidity pension and/or invalidity allowance after state pension age, it will be reduced by the amount of any guaranteed minimum pensions that you get from employers' pension schemes (see pp. 94 and 96).

There are a number of other state benefits which you might qualify for, if you have to retire early because of ill health. They are not covered in this book; you can get details from your local Department of Social Security (see p. 35).

Employers' pension schemes

Choosing to retire early

For schemes set up before 14 March 1989, the tax rules normally prohibit an employer's pension scheme from paying you a full pension before the normal retirement age for the scheme. For these schemes, the earliest normal retirement age allowed by the Inland Revenue is either 50 or 60, depending on when the scheme was set up or when you joined it (see Chapter 5). But, in practice, most schemes set their normal retirement age later than this. For example, the National Association of Pension Funds' survey found that nearly 70 per cent of all schemes covered had a normal retirement age of 65 for men, and three-quarters set the normal age at 60 for women. Virtually all the schemes surveyed set the normal retirement age for men and for women within the range 60 to 65.

Under the tax rules for most pre-March 1989 schemes, the earliest age at which any pension can start to be paid is 50 for men and 45 for women (provided that the woman is within 10 years of normal retirement age). If you voluntarily retire before the normal age for your scheme, the tax rules say that your pension, and other benefits, must be scaled down:

- **retirement pension** This must not exceed one-sixtieth of your final pay for each year that you've worked for the employer *or* the maximum pension can be set by the following formula if this gives a higher amount: your actual years with the employer divided by the number of years (up to a maximum of 40) that you'd have had if you'd stayed until the normal retirement age, multiplied by the maximum pension you could have had based on your final pay now and the years you'd have been with the employer if you'd stayed until retirement. The maximum pension will be reduced in line with any tax-free lump sum taken up
- **tax-free lump sum** Similarly, this is also limited. It must not normally exceed three-eightieths of your final pay for each year you've worked for the employer. But, if it gives a higher amount, it can equal the lump sum you would have got if you'd stayed until normal retirement age (though based on final pay now) scaled down by your actual years of service divided by the number of years (up to 40) to retirement age.

Where the pension and lump sum are worked out by the second method outlined in each case above, the limits will be reduced by the amount of any pension from a previous employer's scheme or from a personal plan.

For schemes set up on, or after, 14 March 1989 – or, if you newly joined an older scheme, on or after 1 June 1989 – new Inland Revenue rules apply to pensions which are paid early. As long as you've reached age 50 at the time you start your early retirement, the rules don't require any reduction in your pension, regardless of the normal retirement age for your scheme. In other words, you can receive the full pension your scheme allows – or even the full pension that the Inland Revenue limits, detailed on pp. 64 to 68, allow.

A scheme set up before 14 March 1989, or an employee joining a scheme before 1 June 1989, can elect to be covered by the new rules, but will also then be covered by other rules applying to post-March 1989 schemes, or post-June 1989 new members – see p. 65.

The Inland Revenue rules, however, merely set a ceiling on benefits. In practice, most schemes pay less generous pensions, and other benefits, in the case of people who choose early retirement. In particular, the scheme is likely to make a reduction to reflect the fact that the pension will probably be paid for a longer period than a pension starting at the normal retirement age. Employers sometimes offer more generous terms where early retirement is at the request of the employer rather than being your independent decision.

You can start to receive a guaranteed minimum pension (GMP) – see Chapter 7 – from an employer's final pay scheme before you reach the state pension age, provided that the pension you receive is not reduced below the amount which must be paid from age 65 (men) or 60 (women). If the pension you would get is less than the GMP due from the state pension age, you won't be able to start taking your pension early.

You can't start to receive a protected rights pension from an employer's money purchase scheme before you've reached state pension age.

EXAMPLE

Ken is 55 and considering early retirement. The normal retirement age for the scheme, which was set up nearly twenty years ago, is 65. Ken has been working for the same employer for the last 15 years and his 'final pay' is £40,000. The tax limits on his pension and lump sum, if he retired now, are:

- **pension** The best of $\frac{1}{60} \times 15 \times £40,000 = £10,000$ and $\frac{15}{25} \times (\frac{40}{60} \times £40,000) = £16,000$. Thus the upper limit on the pension is £16,000 a year (reduced if a lump sum is taken)
- **lump sum** The best of $\frac{3}{80} \times 15 \times £40,000 = £22,500$ and $\frac{15}{25} \times (\frac{72}{80} \times £40,000) = £21,600$. Thus, the maximum lump sum is £22,500.

In practice, the scheme is rather less generous and will provide a maximum pension of only £7,500. Under the scheme rules, part of this can be swapped for a maximum lump sum of £17,500.

Retiring due to ill health

There are no Inland Revenue limits on the age at which you can start to receive your pension, if you have to retire because of ill health. You don't have to be completely incapable of work in order to qualify for an ill health pension – your health may be considered sufficiently bad if it prevents you pursuing your normal work, or if it seriously reduces the amount that you can earn. Each employer's scheme will usually set its own conditions, which may be more rigorous than the Inland Revenue rules, and the scheme will normally require medical evidence of your condition.

The tax limits on the amount of pension you can receive are much more generous than those which apply to voluntary early retirement. The pension and other benefits must not be

145

more than the amounts you could have had if you'd carried on working until normal retirement age (see Chapter 5) but based on your final pay now.

An employer's scheme will usually set its own limits on the level of ill health pension and related benefits, which may restrict the amounts to less than the maximum allowed by the Inland Revenue.

The rules regarding GMPs and protected rights pensions from employers' schemes (see p. 144) also apply in the case of retirement due to ill health.

EXAMPLE

If Ken (see the example on p. 145) were about to retire because of ill health, the maximum pension and lump sum he could have would be:

- **pension** $\frac{40}{60} \times$ £40,000 = £26,667 a year (reduced if a lump sum is taken)
- **lump sum** $\frac{120}{80} \times$ £40,000 = £60,000.

In practice, the scheme sets the benefits below the tax limits. It would pay an ill health pension of £16,667. Under the scheme rules, part of this could be given up for a maximum lump sum of £38,000.

If you were severely ill, and not expected to live for long, the whole of the pension could be converted into a lump sum. There would be a tax charge at a rate of 20 per cent on the part which could not already be taken as a tax-free lump sum. With a small self-administered scheme (see p. 72) the Inland Revenue would need to see medical evidence before payment of the lump sum could be approved.

Personal pension plans

Choosing to retire early

With a new-style personal pension plan, you can't normally choose a pension age of less than 50. With the old-style plans, the earliest age is normally 60; but there's nothing to stop you transferring fròm an old-style plan to a new-style one and then starting your pension before age 60 (though the rest of the new-style plan rules will then apply too – see Chapter 6).

There are no tax rules restricting the pension which you can have in the event of early retirement. But the pension you'll get will generally be lower than a pension which starts to be paid later, because:

- you'll have paid less in contributions
- your investment will have had less time to grow
- your pension will probably be paid for a longer period.

In addition, the plan provider may impose a 'surrender penalty' if you start taking your pension earlier than you'd originally intended. But many plans don't include this type of surrender penalty, so you should be able to avoid these by carefully shopping around at the time you first take out a plan.

You can swap part of your early retirement pension for a tax-free lump sum, subject to the normal rules (see p. 80).

Benefits from a contracted-out personal plan (see Chapter 7) can't be taken before the state pension age of 65 for men or 60 for women, even if you're retiring because of ill health (see below).

Retiring due to ill health

If you have to retire because of ill health, you can start to take a pension from a personal plan at any age. You don't have to be entirely incapable of work but you must be ill to the extent that you're judged permanently incapable of carrying on your normal work, or work of a similar nature for which you're trained or otherwise suited. The plan provider will need medical evidence of your condition.

There are no tax restrictions on the pension you can get. But the problems remain that your pension fund will be smaller because less has been paid in and the investment has had less time to grow, and that your pension will be more expensive because it may have to be paid for longer. There are two 'extras' which can be included in personal pension plans which would help to overcome these problems:

- **waiver of premium benefit**   If you're ill for longer than a given period – say, six months – you no longer have to pay the contributions towards your regular payment plan, but the plan continues to grow as if the contributions had been made and invested. Most personal plans offer this benefit, usually as an option
- **permanent disability insurance**   If you're expected to be permanently incapable of carrying on your work (or similar work) because of ill health or disability, this insurance guarantees that your ill health pension from the plan will be at least a minimum amount. Though this benefit is allowed under the rules for personal plans, it is, in practice, extremely rare.

With both these options, you would have to pay for them by contributing extra towards the plan. The extra amount paid qualifies for tax relief, in the same way as the rest of your contributions. With a new-style personal plan, tax rules prevent more than a quarter of your total contributions being used to provide waiver of premium benefit and permanent disability insurance.

Don't confuse **permanent disability insurance** with **permanent health insurance**. The latter provides you with an income if your earnings stop because of illness, even when the illness is temporary and you're expected to recover from it. Permanent health insurance can't be included within a personal pension plan, and premiums that you pay for permanent health insurance don't qualify for tax relief.

=11=

CHOOSING A
PERSONAL PENSION PLAN

Personal pension plans can be offered by insurance companies, friendly societies, unit trusts, building societies and banks, so there's a huge choice of plan providers and individual plans. Here, we outline the features you might want to look out for; in Chapter 12, we look at the nuts and bolts of taking out a plan and getting advice.

How do you want to save?

Most plan providers offer both regular contribution plans and single lump sum contribution plans. Often, you (or you and your employer, if he's contributing to your plan) have to invest at least a given amount – for example, £20 a month or £200 a year with a regular contribution plan, or £1,000 with a single contribution plan. Most regular contribution plans will accept extra one-off payments, though once again there may be a minimum amount for these – such as £100 or £500.

The majority of regular premium plans will let you increase your contributions if you want to. With some plans you can arrange to increase your payments automatically each year by a set amount, or in line with the index of National Average Earnings (which is published by the government).

An important feature to look out for with a regular premium plan is: can you miss one or more payments without penalty? This can be important if you have a temporary hiccup in your earnings or your circumstances change. You may need to pay a bit extra for a 'waiver of premium' option which allows you to miss payments if your earnings fall because of illness or redundancy, say. Most plan providers also offer plans which will accept just the payments from the government, if you want to use a personal plan just for contracting out of SERPS (see Chapter 7).

Regular payments or lump sum – which is best?

A regular payment plan can be useful in providing an element of discipline in your saving, and in helping you to save a large amount but in manageable chunks. Try to avoid plans which give the pension provider great flexibility to alter adversely (for you) the terms of the plan in future – for example, some plans give the provider enormous scope to increase charges (see p. 155) in future years. You should try to choose a plan which limits the ability of the plan provider to change the terms, or, even better, a plan where the terms are fixed at the time you take it out, if you can find such a plan these days.

On the other hand, you want as much flexibility for yourself as possible – for example, it can be very useful to be able make an extra *ad hoc* payment into the plan if you have a windfall. Equally, it can help to minimise hardship, if you're able occasionally to miss a few contributions without penalty, or reduce the amount you pay. Lump sum plans give you far more flexibility since you just take out a plan whenever you want and have funds available. But you'll have to impose your own discipline on your savings habit. Also, you'll have to accept whatever terms apply to each plan when you take it out, so you can't 'lock into' favourable terms in the way that you may be able to do with a regular payment plan.

Overall, you may pay more in charges (see see p. 155) if you take out a series of lump sum plans than you would have by taking out one regular payment plan. However, regular payment plans will generally penalise you heavily if you stop the plan or transfer it (see Chapter 8) in the early years.

Other things being equal, you may do best by making steady, but possibly modest, contributions to a regular payment plan, but choose one which allows you to make extra one-off payments as and when you can afford them. A generally slightly more costly option would be to have a regular contribution plan as the backbone of your pension saving but take out additional single premium plans when you want to set aside a bit more.

How your money is invested

There are a number of different ways in which the money in your plan can be invested. Some plans *always* invest just one way, others give you a choice. The broad methods of investment are described below.

Choosing your own investments

You build up your own fund of investments comprising assets that you've chosen yourself. Regulations place some limits on your choice but the range is wide and can include UK shares, British Government stocks, and property, among others.

In practice, a 'do-it-yourself' pension plan is likely to be uneconomic unless you have a large sum to invest.

Unit-linked plans and unit trusts

Unit-linked plans are offered by many insurance companies and some friendly societies. Unit trusts offer similar plans. Your money is allocated to units whose value is linked to a specific fund of investments. With a unit trust, your money buys units in a pool of investments. With both, your return depends on the price of your units; this rises and falls in line with the value of the underlying investments.

There are different types of investment fund and unit trust, investing in, for example, UK shares, foreign shares, British Government stocks, and so on. A managed fund or mixed unit trust invests in a broad spread of different investments.

You can usually choose to invest in more than one fund at once, but there may be a minimum investment for each one. Generally, you can switch between the different funds or different trusts after you've started the plan.

With-profits plans

These are offered by insurance companies and friendly societies. Your money is invested by the plan provider in a broad spread of investments – shares, British Government stocks, property, and so on. Your return depends largely on how well the investments grow, but also on other factors, such as the provider's profits from other parts of his business, his level of expenses, and the policy on distributing profits.

Your return is in the form of bonuses: **reversionary bonuses** are added to your plan at regular intervals – often, yearly; a **terminal bonus** is usually added at the time you convert your investment fund into pension. Once added, bonuses can't be taken away, so the amount in your plan can never fall. But the level of future bonuses isn't guaranteed. Plan providers are usually cautious about increasing reversionary bonuses, and reluctant to cut them. But the level of terminal bonus can vary greatly, and can amount to a sizeable proportion of your plan – as much as half in some cases.

Unitised with-profits plans

These are similar to with-profits plans. They are offered by insurance companies and can either be a separate plan, or an option within a unit-linked plan.

Your money is allocated to units in the with-profits fund. The amount of your capital can't fall, and it can grow in two ways: the value of units is increased throughout each year in line with a declared bonus, or growth, rate – this is similar to the reversionary bonuses you get under a with-profits plan. In addition, a terminal bonus may be added at the time you take your pension.

Deposit-based schemes and deposit-administration plans

Deposit-based schemes are offered by some building societies. Deposit administration plans – which are becoming rare these days – are similar but are offered mainly by insurance companies. A cash fund or money market fund as an option within a unit-linked plan is similar. Your money is invested in an account to which interest is periodically added. The amount of your capital can't fall and grows as the interest is added, but the level of future interest rates isn't guaranteed.

Which type of plan?

Your choice of investment depends largely on how much risk you're willing to take, and the length of time to go until you need your pension. In general, to have the chance of a higher return, you'll need to take more risk. Unit-linked plans and unit trusts, where the amount of your investment can fall as well as rise, are more risky than with-profits plans, where your investment increases but can't fall back. Deposit-based, and deposit administration, plans are generally viewed as the least risky, since the amount of your capital can't fall, and because interest rates tend to be more steady than the terminal bonus rates on with-profits policies. But the deposit-type plans will tend to give the lowest returns.

The value of a unit-linked plan or unit trust, and the level of bonuses from a with-profits plan are linked to a pool of underlying investments. Chart 11 overleaf shows that an underlying investment, such as shares, has shown quite violent short-term swings in the return it gives, but has beaten inflation over the long term. By contrast, the return from interest-earning deposits, such as a building society account, has historically fallen short of inflation for long periods. Chart 11 covers the period 1960 to 1989. Over that time, £1,000 invested by a basic rate taxpayer in the building society account would have *fallen* to just £560 after taking

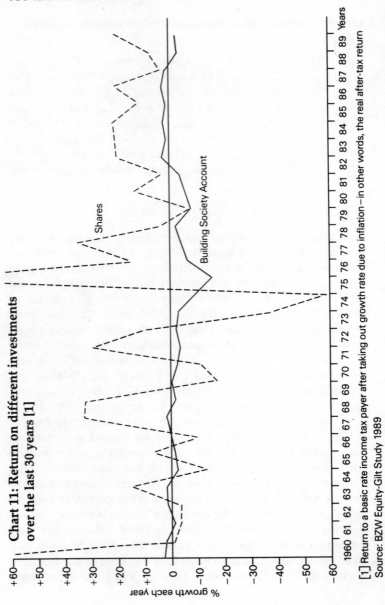

Chart 11: Return on different investments over the last 30 years [1]

[1] Return to a basic rate income tax payer after taking out growth rate due to inflation – in other words, the real after-tax return

Source: BZW Equity-Gilt Study 1989

inflation into account. But £1,000 invested in shares would have grown to nearly £3,200, after basic rate tax, on top of the growth needed to keep pace with inflation. If you put long-term savings into a deposit-based (or deposit-administration) plan, it's likely that the buying power of your investment will fall.

It's essential that long-term retirement savings should be invested so that their value at least keeps pace with inflation. If you're a long way from retirement, you should probably be looking mainly at unit-linked and unit trust investments, as these give you the best chance of beating inflation and of getting a good return over the long term. Choosing a managed fund or mixed trust is less risky than going for more specialised funds or trusts. If you prefer a lower risk strategy, or you are within, say, 10 or 15 years of retirement, you might consider investing part of your money on a unit-linked or unit trust basis and part on a with-profits basis. When you're within a few years of retirement, deposit-based schemes (and deposit-administration plans) can be a possible way of protecting your past investment growth from falls in stock market prices – most unit-linked plans include a money fund, or cash fund, which can be used in a similar way.

Fees and charges

With deposit-based schemes, the rate of interest usually partly reflects the expenses incurred by the plan provider, though occasionally there are separate charges that you must pay – for example, an administration fee. Similarly, the level of bonuses earned under a with-profits plan incorporates an allowance for expenses – though again you may have to pay a separate policy fee or administration charge as well.

The position with unit-linked plans, unit trusts and unitised with-profits plans is quite different: there are generally few hidden expenses. Instead you pay a variety of explicit charges. Unit trust charges are relatively simple, but

Table 29: Charges for unit-linked and unit trust plans

Name of the charge	Description
Charges used with both unit-linked and unit trust plans	
Bid-offer spread	The difference between the higher offer price at which you are allocated or buy units and the lower bid price at which you cash them in. Typically, the spread will be around 6%
Management charge	A yearly charge set against the investment fund or unit trust to cover the costs of managing the underlying investments. Typically, this might be about 1% or 1.5% of the amount of the fund or trust
One-off admin-istration charge	There might be a single charge at the outset of the plan, or deducted from the first year's payments
Additional charges with unit-linked plans	
Policy fee and/or administration charge	A deduction made at regular intervals to cover the costs of the paperwork, etc., involved in setting up and running the plan
Unit allocation	A given percentage of each payment is allocated to units. The percentage may be lower in the earlier years of the plan, and it may be lower if you pay monthly, say, rather than yearly. Don't be misled by allocations of over 100%: it sounds as if you're being credited with more money than you've paid in but this isn't so – it may mean 100% of the money left after a policy fee or administration charge has been deducted, or you may be getting a refund of part of the management fee
Capital units	You may be allocated 'special' units, especially in the first year or two of the plan, which have a much higher management charge – for example 3% or 5% of the amount of the fund. You usually carry on paying this higher charge throughout the life of the plan
Surrender charges	You're likely to be credited with only part of the value of your plan if you stop paying into it, or transfer it, in the early years

Note: unit-linked plans may charge you if you switch your contributions and/or invested money from one fund to another, though the first switch, or two, each year is usually free. Switching unit trusts will be expensive, if you have to sell units in one trust and buy units in another. But some unit trust plans make use of 'umbrella funds' – the trust is split into a number of different funds between which you can switch either free or at low cost the plans offered by insurance companies often have a very complicated charging structure. Table 29 opposite summarises the charges you may come across.

Transferring your plan before retirement

You don't have to contribute to the same plan until retirement. You can stop contributing but leave the money which has already built up invested in the plan. Alternatively, you can transfer your money to another personal plan or to an employer's pension scheme, if the plan or scheme agrees to accept the transfer.

All personal plans must give you the right to take a transfer, but watch out in case there are penalties for stopping the plan early. These might take the form of surrender charges (see Table 29), or you might be losing the right to a 'loyalty' bonus paid only if you continue the plan for a set period or until retirement. Surrender charges are often very severe if you stop or transfer a plan in the early years – the value of your plan may be less than the amount paid in contributions and, in extreme cases, the plan may be worth nothing at all.

When can you retire?

The tax rules normally allow you to take the proceeds of a new-style personal pension plan at any age from 50 to 75. But protected rights from a contracted-out plan (see Chapter 7) can't be taken before state pension age (65 for men and 60 for women). Within these limits, the plan may set its own rules.

With some plans, you have to choose a retirement date at the time you first take out the plan, though there will be no penalty if you retire after that date. But there may be a penalty if you choose to retire earlier, so it's probably best to choose the earliest possible date at the outset even if you subsequently change your mind. Many plans don't insist on a set retirement date, but let you choose near the time.

Retiring at 50 may seem like an attractive option, but in practice it might not be feasible. The size of your pension will depend largely on how much you invest, how the investment grows, and how much pension you can 'buy' with your fund. If you retire early, you'll have invested less, your fund will have had less time to grow, and you'll be using the fund to buy more years of pension. If you plan to retire early, you should be prepared to save more and from an earlier age than if you're aiming for a later retirement.

You don't have to stop work to be able to take a pension from a personal plan. This means that you could ease back on work but maintain your income by starting to take a pension before you fully retire. Having several personal plans with different pension ages adds to your retirement flexibility.

Pension choices

There are different types of pension that you can choose: a level pension, one which increases by a set amount each year, or one which increases in line with price inflation. Your pension can also be guaranteed to be paid for a certain number of years, in case death occurs within that period. Different plan providers also offer different terms for providing widows', widowers' and children's pensions, if you are the one to die first after the pension has started.

You don't have to make your choice about these features at the time you take out the plan, as long as you choose a plan which gives you an **open market option** – most do. This allows you to take your fund to another plan provider (which must be an insurance company or friendly society) at the time you want to start taking your pension. So you can leave your shopping around for a pension until then. However, at the time you start the plan, you should check whether there will be any penalty if you exercise your open market option at retirement. For example, a penalty might be in the form of a

retirement bonus which you get only if you stay with the original plan provider. Contracted-out personal plans (see Chapter 7) must, by law, give you an open-market option.

Life insurance

If you're eligible to take out a personal pension plan, you're also eligible to take out a special term insurance policy, called a **section 621 policy**. This is a protection-only policy which provides a lump sum or income for your dependants in the event of your death. Unlike other forms of term insurance, you get tax relief at your top rate of tax on the premiums you pay.

You don't have to take out a section 621 policy with the same company or society that provides your pension plan, and you can take out such a policy even if you don't take out a pension plan. For further details about section 621 policies, see p. 138.

Comparing pension plans

Once you've settled on the broad type of plan that you want and the features you need, you'll generally still be left with a choice of different plan providers. Unfortunately, there's no easy way to choose between them.

Plan providers, and most advisers, make much of the past investment performance of particular providers. There's no doubt that investment performance is likely to be the single most important factor in determining how much pension you receive. But, sadly, there seems to be no reliable way of predicting in advance which plan providers will perform best – especially when you're looking at very long-term investments, such as pensions. Many studies have been carried out, in universities and business schools in Britain and in America, which have found no relationship at all between past investment performance and future performance.

159

Despite the evidence, you're likely to find that the invest-ment track record of a plan provider is the feature which is often stressed more heavily than any other. But you should also look at other factors. These might include:

- **financial strength** What reserves does the plan provider have? Reserves are a bit like the 'emergency fund' you probably keep handy in the building society in case times become hard. A plan provider needs sufficient reserves to guard against going bust, and the law specifies minimum reserve levels for the various plan providers. But going bust is an extreme situation. You need to consider financial strength in another light: a provider may be giving its investors good returns now, but can they keep it up? For example, are they dipping into reserves to keep up bonus rates – this is a bit like selling the family silver to pay the gas bill. Is there a risk that investment returns will be cut in future, or that charges will have to be increased?
- **expense levels and charges** Very few plan providers offer plans with charges that are fixed for the life of the plan. With some plans, there is an upper limit above which charges can't rise, but with many there's no ceiling speci-fied. And, where there are no explicit charges, the expenses which influence the interest rate or bonus rate, can usually vary without limit. So it's a good idea to have a look at how efficiently the plan provider manages its business – does it run up high expenses, or are they relatively low?
- **investment philosophy** Higher-risk investments tend to give higher returns over the long term, but risky invest-ments can go badly wrong. A 'safer' investment strategy may give a steadier return, but the results over the long term may be relatively poor. What approach does the plan provider take?
- **other factors** How is the plan provider's business orga-nised – as a company with shareholders to consider and as a source of business capital, or as a mutual organisation owned by its investors? Is it part of a larger group, does it have a foreign parent, to what extent can it draw on the

resources of the rest of the group or of the parent company? Is it involved in other types of business, are these quite separate from the pensions business, could the organisation be vulnerable to bad spells in its other activities, or do the other activities enhance the strength of the organisation? Is the business growing, static, or declining, is the organisation eager to compete for pensions customers?

It used to be very difficult for the individual to get any information about these sorts of factors. Proposed changes in the law should mean that insurance companies offering with-profits plans will have to make available much more information of this sort. The proposal is that they should produce a company booklet giving facts and figures about the company's with-profits business. The booklet would be available on request.

The law-makers hope that other plan providers will follow suit and provide booklets not just for their with-profits plans, but for other types of plans, too. Even if this happens, for most people the information will be fairly difficult to use and interpret; but a good financial adviser should be able to help. At present, however, there is a dearth of information easily available to the investor. If you have the time and inclination, you can glean information from specialist magazines, such as *Planned Savings* and *Money Management*. Alternatively, you could consult a financial adviser (see Chapter 12).

More information

If you're already interested in the plans offered by particular providers, you can get information about the plans direct from them. The telephone book may have the address and phone number of a local branch or office. If not, your local library should be able to find details of the head office for you.

Specialist magazines are a useful source of information about plans generally and of surveys comparing the different plans which are available. An added advantage is that surveys usually give details of how to contact the providers for more information. Some magazines are available through newsagents. With many, you can arrange a subscription, or obtain single copies, direct from the publisher. Specialist magazines which run regular surveys of pension plans are: *Planned Savings*, United Trade Press Ltd (see address on p. 215); *Money Management* and *Pensions Management*, FT Business Publishing (see address on p. 213). A survey of personal pension plans, which is updated regularly, is also contained in: *Choose Your Pension, An Action Pack from Which?*, Consumers' Association (see address on p. 213).

═══12═══

SHOPPING FOR A PERSONAL PLAN

You can buy a personal pension plan either direct from the plan provider or through a middleman. There are three types of middleman:

- **direct salespeople**   These are individuals who work for a single plan provider and sell the products of just that provider
- **tied agents**   These are individuals or firms who are selling the services of just one company
- **independent advisers**   These can sell the full range of products available from all the companies in the market.

When you first have contact with a middleman, they should provide you with a buyer's guide, which explains what type of middleman they are, and what type of service they can give you.

Before you do business with any plan provider, salesperson, agent or adviser, you should check their credentials. All personal pension plans – except deposit-type plans sold, for example, by some building societies – count as investments under the Financial Services Act 1986. That Act requires that anyone advising about, or selling, investments must be **authorised** (or directly connected – for example, as employee – to someone else who is authorised). To get authorisation, a firm must be 'fit and proper' to carry on their investment business and must be financially sound. A business which carries on investment business in the UK without authorisation is committing a criminal offence.

An investment business can be authorised directly by the

Securities and Investments Board (SIB), which is the official body that oversees the running of the Financial Services Act, or through one of the bodies to which the SIB has delegated some of its powers. These bodies are the five Self-Regulating Organisations (SROs) and the Recognised Professional Bodies (RPBs).

If you're .considering pension plans that fall within the scope of the Act, you should not have any dealings with a business which is not authorised. If you come across such a business, or are uncertain about its status, you should report it to the SIB (see address on p. 215).

The SIB keeps a Register of authorised investment businesses. It gives you details of the authorising body, the status of the business, the types of products it deals in and the address of the business. Before you deal with a plan provider or adviser, you should check their entry in the Register: if they are not listed, they are not authorised. Make sure that the Register entry shows that they are authorised for the type of business you propose to do with them.

You can check the SIB Register by writing to the Information Office, SIB (see address on p. 215) or by telephoning a special number for Register enquiries: 071-929 3652. Alternatively, you can consult the Register directly using **Prestel** – an electronic information system. Prestel is available in most main libraries, and the library staff will be able to help you use it.

Dealing with a plan provider or a salesperson

Getting in touch

You might decide to deal directly with the plan provider if, say, you've been satisfied doing business with them before, or if you've picked them out from a published survey of the market (see p. 161). You might get in touch with a company direct in response to an advertisement in the press.

Literature from the company will give you an address and phone number you can contact. A published survey will often include contact details. Otherwise, you may find the address of a local branch in the telephone book. Failing all these, most public libraries have one or more business directories which will give you the details of the head office.

It's a good idea to get details from two or three plan providers at this stage, so that you can compare them in detail, fully check what the plans offer, their charges and so on, and select the most suitable one for you. The plan provider will usually arrange a meeting with one of their salespeople either at their premises, or at your home.

The selling process

In the case of pension plans from life insurance companies, friendly societies and unit trusts, there are regulations under the Financial Services Act 1986 which are aimed at protecting you from bad or dishonest selling practices. One of the most important regulations is the 'know your customer' rule: the salesperson must gather enough information about you and your circumstances to put them in a position to assess your needs and to decide whether or not the products they have to sell are suitable for you. If you're looking at pension plans, this means that the adviser should – as a minimum – find out about the following areas:

- your age and sex
- your employment status
- your earnings
- your tax position
- your state of health
- whether you have a husband or wife
- whether you have children, and their ages
- your regular financial commitments (such as mortgage payments, household bills, and so on) and your likely commitments in retirement
- your intended retirement age

165

- your likely entitlement to state pensions
- details of any employer's pension scheme that is open to you
- details of any previous employer's schemes from which you're entitled to a pension at retirement
- details of any personal plans that you have
- details of any life insurance you currently have
- details of any other savings and investments
- how much you can afford to pay into a pension plan
- whether you want to transfer any funds from previous pension schemes or plans into a new plan
- what features you want your plan to have
- your attitude towards investment risk.

The only situation in which less information would be sufficient is where your intention is only to contract out through a rebate-only plan (see Chapter 7). In this case, the plan provider needs to know your age and sex, employment status, earnings, details of any employer's scheme open to you, and your attitude towards investment risk.

Once the salesperson has got to know you, he must give you 'best advice' about the company's products. He must recommend to you the most suitable of the company's wares or, if none are suitable, he must tell you that. He should help you to make your decision in the light of the options open to you. This means, for example, that if you could join an excellent employer's scheme and it would be unlikely that a personal plan could beat it, the salesperson should tell you that none of his products are suitable for you. In practice, the position is not so clear cut: though there are strict regulations about how the benefits from a personal plan are to be estimated (see p. 174), there are no corresponding rules for illustrating the benefits from employers' schemes. If the salesperson tends towards a pessimistic attitude to your employer's scheme, a personal plan could look more attractive than it would appear given different assumptions.

A salesperson for one company within a group of related companies might be unable to sell the full range of that group's products. If he recognises that the product of another company within the group might be suitable, he can offer to arrange for you to meet with a salesperson for that other company. For example, a life insurance salesperson might arrange contact with the unit trust arm of the same group.

A salesperson for one company can't recommend the products of another company. In the rather unlikely event that, on your own initiative, you asked the salesperson to arrange for you to buy the products of an entirely different company, the salesperson could do this on what's called an **execution-only** basis – he would act merely as a channel for your business, but could not advise or comment on it.

When you have agreed to a deal, you'll be given or sent detailed information about the product. You'll also receive a **cancellation notice** which tells you that you have the right to withdraw from the deal within 14 days of receiving the notice. After 14 days, you're committed to the contract.

Unfortunately, the Financial Services Act does not apply to deposit-type personal pension plans, such as those offered by some building societies. They are covered by regulations overseen by the Department of Social Security, but these are scant compared with the Financial Services Act. In particular, a provider offering just deposit-type plans does not have to 'know you as a customer' or give you 'best advice'.

Doorstep selling

You might also find yourself in contact with a salesperson as the result of a **cold call**. This is when a salesperson telephones, or appears on your doorstep, out of the blue. Personal pension plans offered by life insurance companies, friendly societies and unit trusts can be sold in this way. There are strict regulations which apply to such calls, including:

- the salesperson should introduce himself, make clear the company he represents, and that he is unable to sell the

products of any other company. If the call is a personal
visit, he should give you his business card
- the salesperson should make clear the reason for the visit,
and establish whether or not you wish the call to continue.
If you don't, he must respect your wishes and end the call
- he must respect your right to end the call at any time
- if, at the time of the call, you agree to invest in a product,
you must be sent subsequently a cancellation notice (see
p. 167) which gives you 14 days within which you can back
out of the deal.

Despite the regulations, a cold call can be an unwelcome,
and even distressing, intrusion. The salesperson is there in
the hope of making a sale and will have been trained in all
sorts of persuasive techniques, so you're right to be wary.
You should bear in mind the following points:

- if you're not interested in the products, don't be afraid to
end the call – as a last resort, you can simply hang up the
telephone or close the door
- if you are interested, but would prefer to consider the
product in peace and in your own time, ask the salesperson
to give you, or post to you, the relevant literature, and say
you'll be in touch with him if you want to pursue the matter
further. If he won't agree, hang up or close the door
- if you're interested and want the call to continue, invite the
salesperson in, but remember that however friendly he is,
this is basically someone who wants your business. The
salesperson is not your guest, and if he becomes too
persistent you will have to be inhospitable
- if you like the product, don't sign up there and then. It may
well be the best product for you, but you can't be sure until
you've compared it with other products which are available. Also, you should pause to make sure that you really
want it, and that you can afford it. It's best to ignore the
temptation of discounts and free gifts if you sign straight-
away. You could pay dearly in the long run for a hasty
decision made now, particularly with a long-term investment such as a pension plan

- if you do agree to a deal at the time of the call, remember that you have a cooling-off period within which you can change your mind. Make use of that period to check that the product really is one that you want.

Going to a tied agent

Getting in touch

You'll see tied agents' advertisements in, say, local newspapers, trade directories and the *Yellow Pages*. Often, a tied agent will make the initial contact through a cold call (see p. 167) or by posting literature to you. You may be on an agent's mailing list as a result of having shown interest in other of their products, or you may be on a mailing list which the agent has bought from an outside source.

You'll also find tied agents in your high street. They may include bank and building society branches, and small firms operating under a variety of names, such as 'insurance and pensions adviser', 'insurance consultant', 'pensions consultant', 'insurance broker', 'financial adviser', and so on.

The selling process

The Financial Services Act prohibits a middleman from advising on and selling the products of a handful of companies; the middleman must either sell the wares of *one* company or deal in the full range of products on the market. This regulation was made to stop the misleading, and previously fairly common, practice of an investment adviser appearing to give independent advice about the whole market when in reality they were channelling all the business to just a few companies.

Unfortunately, there's no requirement for tied agents to display their status on their shopfronts, so you might not be aware of it until you're inside. If you don't want tied advice, or don't want to invest in the products of the particular company to whom the agent is tied, don't be afraid to leave without discussing your business.

The status of bank and building society branches can be particularly confusing. A few building societies have their own pension products, but most societies sell the pension plans of others – usually insurance companies. A few building societies act as independent advisers, but most are tied to a single plan provider. The position of the banks is similar; the main difference is that some of the bigger banks have their own insurance company arm whose products they sell through their branches. But to complicate matters, some banks and building societies give tied advice through their branches, but also have a separate operation which gives independent advice; in this situation a branch can't itself give independent advice, but it can direct customers to the independent arm, or even act as a channel for independent advice as long as it makes no comment on the advice. In some cases, the independent route is pointed out only to customers who have relatively large sums to invest.

Tied agents are regulated by the same rules that apply to a company's own salespeople (see pp. 165 to 169), and the company is ultimately responsible for the conduct of its agents. If you deal with a tied agent, they must make clear to you their status and the company that they represent. They must follow the 'know your customer' and 'best advice' rules, and tied agents who 'cold call' are bound by the regulations outlined on p. 167. If you invest through a tied agent, the plan provider will send you details of the product and a cancellation notice (see p. 167), giving you 14 days within which you can back out of the deal.

Going to an independent adviser

Getting in touch

Local newspapers, trade directories and the *Yellow Pages* may carry advertisements for independent advisers. You may also find some trading in the high street. The titles – 'pensions consultant', 'insurance broker', 'financial adviser', and so on – are often the same as those used by tied agents. Look out for the term 'independent' and also for a round logo with the letters 'IFA'. 'IFA' stands for Independent Financial Adviser and the logo can be used only by independent advisers who have joined IFA Promotion Ltd. This is an organisation set up by a group of insurance companies specifically to provide support and publicity for independent financial advisers. Not all independent advisers have chosen to join IFA Promotion Ltd, so the absence of the logo doesn't necessarily mean that a business is not independent. IFA Promotion Ltd can provide you with a list of its members in your area if you telephone 081-200 3000.

Many accountants, solicitors and actuaries give financial advice. They are all independent advisers in accordance with the rules governing their professions.

The selling process

As the name suggests, independent advisers must be independent of any particular company and must base their advice on the products of the full range of companies in the market.

An independent adviser is bound by the 'know your customer' rule, explained on p. 165, and you should expect them to investigate all the areas outlined there. An independent adviser must also give you 'best advice'. In theory, this means that they must recommend the most suitable product for you from the range available. In practice, the rule is applied less strictly: the adviser must make regular surveys of the market to identify the best products but doesn't need to make a special survey for each customer; and the adviser is allowed to identify the 'best' product for an identifiable group of customers – for example, all people in a given age group who want rebate-only pension plans – rather than seeking out a product afresh each time a customer comes along.

If you invest through an adviser, the plan provider will

send you details of the plan and a cancellation notice – see p. 167. You have 14 days within which you can back out of the deal.

Once again, the Financial Services Act regulations don't apply to deposit-type plans.

How salespeople and advisers are paid

Salespeople employed by a particular company may be paid by salary, bonuses, commission on sales, fringe benefits such as a car, and so on. Tied agents usually receive commissions on the sales that they make, and they may be able to claim back from the company certain expenses associated with running the business. Many independent advisers receive commission on the sales that they make and, in one way or another, the commission payments are met out of the investment to which you agree. Some agents and advisers charge you a fee for their services and, in this case, commissions they receive may be used to reduce the fee you pay, or the commissions may be paid over to you. Solicitors and accountants always charge fees but may keep any commissions they receive only with your consent.

Payment by commission raises the possibility of some conflict of interest. The biggest potential problem is with independent advisers. Plan providers compete for the clients of independent advisers, in part, by offering better commission deals than their rivals. Yet, the adviser who is your agent and is, in any case, bound by the 'best advice' rule, is supposed to advise you with reference only to your circumstances – not to the amount of commission they'll earn. There is clearly a temptation for an independent adviser to recommend the products of the company that will pay them the most commission. Some plan providers don't pay commission to the middleman at all, so there's a risk that the plans of these providers might be overlooked.

Salespeople and tied agents are, of course, able to sell only the products of one company. But the temptation of commission payments could persuade them – as well as independent advisers – to recommend their customers to invest more than they really wanted to, or to recommend a higher-commission product in preference to one which might be more suitable for the customer.

You should be on your guard against these problems. Work out for yourself how much you want to invest, make sure that you know what you want from a product and check that the recommended one meets your requirements.

If you use a solicitor or accountant, the problems are less likely to arise because they are bound by the rules of their professions to tell you what commission will be paid to them and, in any case, they can't keep the commission unless you've agreed to that happening. If you're using most other types of independent adviser, you won't necessarily be aware of the commission payment until late in your transaction with the adviser. You'll be sent written details of the amount, or percentage rate, of commission an adviser will receive when the plan provider sends you the full details of the product you've chosen. But these details are sent out after you've agreed the deal, and though you have the 14 days' cancellation period, you're unlikely to alter your choice at that late stage merely because the adviser's commission earnings look a bit high. Instead of waiting, it's a good idea to ask at the time you're discussing the deal with your adviser how much commission he stands to earn – an adviser does not have to volunteer this information but *must* provide it *if you ask.*

It's not easy to judge what level of commission is reasonable, but if you're discussing several plans – and with more than one adviser – you'll be alerted to any particularly high payments that might be swaying the recommendation. Eventually, it's expected that the press – for example, the specialist magazines noted on p. 162 – might carry surveys of the levels of commission paid throughout the industry.

Independent advisers don't have to tell you what commission, if any, they receive through recommending deposit-type plans, such as those offered by some building societies.

Advertisements

The Financial Services Act lays down comprehensive rules to control the way investments are advertised. These include:

- an advertisement must give the name of the advertiser and, usually, the name of the regulating body (see p. 164), too
- the nature of the investment must be clear. If full details are not given, the advertisement must say how you can get them
- references to past performance mustn't be misleading, and there must be a warning that past performance isn't necessarily a guide to the future
- projections and illustrations, if used, must be based on standardised growth rates and charges (see below)
- if the value of your investment can go down as well as up – for example, as with unit-linked investments and unit trusts – there must be a warning to this effect.

Projections and illustrations

When you've given details of your circumstances and needs to a plan provider, agent, or intermediary, the plan provider will produce an illustration showing you what pension and other benefits the plan *might* produce by your selected retirement age – or by the state pension age in the case of rebate-only plans (see Chapter 7). Illustrations are essential tools in your pension planning because they give you a guide to the amount that you need to save, but they should be treated with caution for two reasons. Firstly, an illustration must be based on *assumptions* – educated guesses or estimates – about factors such as future investment performance, a company's expenses, plan charges, and so on. The Financial Services Act rules lay down set assumptions which must be used. Secondly, except in the case of rebate-only plans, illustrations tell you what you'll get in terms of *future* money. The amounts seem very large, but the buying power of each £1 of future money is almost certainly going to be a lot less than the buying power of £1 today (see p. 15). So you must adjust the figures for the likely effect of future inflation before an illustration can be of much use to you. The Financial Services Act requires that you be given a standard note explaining about inflation, but the calculations are not easy for the average person, so ask the plan provider, the agent, or your adviser to do the sums for you.

As the law requires that standard assumptions are used when making illustrations, all plan providers will quote the same figures for the same sort of plan and a given client. So illustrations can't be any help in comparing one provider's plan with that of another.

The four Guides on the next four pages show you how to interpret a pension plan illustration for a rebate-only plan and for a plan to which you contribute directly.

If things go wrong

Contact the company

If you have a complaint about your plan, the plan provider, or the advice you were given, you should first contact the manager of the plan provider or the financial adviser with whom you dealt. If you're not satisfied with the response from them and they are part of a larger organisation, you should take your complaint to the head office – the branch can tell you who to contact, or you can get details from a business directory at most public libraries.

An advisory service

The Occupational Pensions Advisory Service is a voluntary body which was originally set up to help people who were having problems concerning their employer's pension scheme. It now has a wider remit and offers its services to those having problems with their personal pension plans. The service won't make any judgments about your case, but

Part 1: Investing the DSS contribution

① **Personal Pension Plan**
(secured by DSS 'protected rights' contributions)

② **Unit-Linked Fund**

③ **Date** 4 June 1990

④ Male **aged under** 31 years as at 1 May 1990

⑤ **Pension age for illustration 65**

The contributions paid by the DSS £1338 . . . . ⑥

This contribution is calculated on the basis that for the purposes of determining the the DSS 'protected rights' contribution, earnings of £20000 are received uniformly during the year ending 5 April 1991

⑥ The above contribution includes a 2.00% incentive payment from the DSS.

The benefits on survival to the illustrated pension age

		Fund	
Projected fund if future real rate of return is:	½% p.a.	£ 1452	(see note 2)
	2½% p.a.	£ 2893	(see note 2)

⑦

Projected transfer values to other pension contracts

The plan may be discontinued at any time and the benefits secured transferred to another pension provider. The projected transfer values at each of the first 5 anniversaries of the commencement of the plan are shown in the table below.

Number of complete years in force	Projected transfer values (see note 3)
1	£1396
2	£1529
3	£1675
4	£1836
5	£2011

⑧ · · · · · · · · · · · · · ·

Please see notes

1 This part shows what pension you might get by investing the rebate and incentive for the 1990–91 tax year. Even if you make extra contributions yourself, the rebate-only part of your plan must be illustrated separately. **2** How your contributions will be invested. **3** Date on which the illustration was prepared. **4** The illustration is for a man now aged 30. **5** You can't take this part of your pension before you reach state pension age. **6** This is the National Insurance rebate for the 1990–91 tax year (including basic rate tax relief) plus the 2% incentive (see Chapter 7). **7** These are projections of the fund that might have grown by retirement. The fund will be used to 'buy' your pension. The projections are based on standard assumptions, and they show growth *on top of* inflation – i.e. the projected funds are given in terms of today's money (see Chapter 1). **8** Under the Financial Services Act, your illustration must show estimates of the transfer value (see Chapter 8) of your plan for each of the first five years. They have not been reduced to take account of the effect of inflation.

Using a personal pension fund
built up from contributions paid
by the DSS ('protected rights')
to buy a pension

Protected Rights Annuity .... ①
(under a personal pension scheme)

Date 4 June 1990

Male **aged under** 31 years as at 1 May 1990

Pension age for illustration
  Annuitant aged over 65

Purchase price   a) £1452   b) £2893
  being the projected funds available under a personal pension scheme

Benefits
  Initial gross annuity   a) £9 per month   b) £22 per month .... ②

	Projected gross payments on survival (see notes below)	
After 5 years	£10	£26
After 10 years	£12	£30
After 15 years	£14	£34 .... ③
After 20 years	£16	£40
After 25 years	£19	£46

The annuity payments shown above are amounts per month.

The annuity will be payable by monthly instalments, the first falling due on the first day of the month following the date of purchase and the last on the due date preceding the death of the annuitant or, if the annuitant was married at the time of death, the due date preceding the death of the annuitant's spouse. On the annuitant's death leaving a spouse surviving, the gross annuity will reduce by one-half of that previously payable. The annuity will increase annually at 3% p.a. compound, the first increase falling due one year after payment of the first instalment.

This illustration is based on the assumptions as set out in the attached personal pension plan illustration which must be read in conjunction with this illustration.

④

Please see notes · · · · · · · · · · · · · · · ·

1 This bit of the illustration shows the 'protected rights' pension you'd get using the fund built up by investing the DSS contribution. All of that fund must be used to buy pension, which increases by 3% a year, plus a widow's or widower's pension. None of it can be taken as a tax-free lump sum.   **2** Financial Services Act rules say what annuity rate must be used to convert your retirement fund into pension for the purposes of the illustration. This is not a guarantee, and the rate used when you come to retire could be higher or lower.   **3** Financial Services Act rules say that you must be shown what the pension would be after every fifth year. The amounts are in terms of today's buying power, so look deceptively small compared with other pension projections. For comparison, some illustrations would also show here the amount of SERPS pension you'd be giving up for the year (currently about £5 a month in this example).   **4** The illustration will be accompanied by explanatory notes, and possibly other literature. **It's important that you read the notes and other material.**

Part 2: Investing your own (and possibly your employer's) contributions

① **Personal Pension Plan**
  Unit-Linked Fund

② **Date** 4 June 1990

  Male **aged under** 31 years as at 1 May 1990 . . . . ③

  Pension age for illustration 65 . . . . ④

  The contributions

A monthly contribution of	£100.00
Less income tax saved if at **25.00% of the contributions** ⑤	£25.00
Net initial outlay	£75.00 . . . . ⑥

  The benefits on survival
  to the illustrated pension age

	Projected benefits if future rate of return is	
	8½% p.a.	13% p.a. . . . . ⑦
Projected fund	£ 196000	£ 542000
which could provide ⑧ **(a) projected tax-free cash sum** **(see note)**	£ 49000	£ 135000
plus (b) projected balance of fund	£ 147000	£ 407000

  The balance of the fund not providing a tax-free cash sum must be used to purchase a pension.

  Projected transfer values to other pension contracts

  The plan may be discontinued at any time and the benefits secured transferred to another pension provider. The projected transfer values at each of the first 5 anniversaries of the commencement of the plan are shown in the table below.

Number of complete years in force	Projected transfer values (see note)
1	£1201
2	£2520
⑨ 3	£3981
4	£5578
5	£7331

  Please see notes

1 How your contributions will be invested. **2** Date on which the illustration was prepared. **3** The illustration is for a man now aged 30. **4** You can usually choose the age at which you want to start your pension, provided it lies between ages 50 and 75 (inclusive). **5** You get tax relief on your contributions at your highest rate (see Chapter 6). **6** If you're an employee, this is the amount you hand over to the plan provider. They add basic rate tax relief to your plan (see Chapter 6). If you're self-employed, you hand over the full £100 and claim the tax relief yourself. **7** These are projections of the fund that might have grown by retirement. They are based on standard assumptions. The amounts seem large because they have not been reduced to take account of the effect of inflation – remember that the buying power will be much lower than this (see Chapter 1). **8** Part of the fund can be taken as a tax-free lump sum, the rest as pension. **9** Under the Financial Services Act, your illustration must show estimates of the transfer value (see Chapter 8) of your plan for each of the first five years.

178

Using a personal pension fund to buy a pension

Without-Profits Annuity .... ①
(under a personal pension scheme)

Date 4 June 1990

Male **aged under** 31 years as at 1 May 1990

Pension age for illustration
Male **aged over** 65 years

Purchase price   (a) £147000   (b) £407000
being the projected funds available under a personal pension scheme.

Benefits   ②
Initial gross annuity   (a) £1400.00 per month   (b) £4400.00 per month

Projected gross payments on survival

③ After 5 years   (a) £1400 per month   (b) £4400 per month
    After 10 years   (a) £1400   (b) £4400
    After 15 years   (a) £1400   (b) £4400
    After 20 years   (a) £1400   (b) £4400
    After 25 years   (a) £1400   (b) £4400

The annuity payments shown above are amounts per month.

The annuity will be payable by monthly instalments, the first falling due on the first day of the month following the date of purchase and the last on the due date preceding the death of the annuitant or the death of the survivor of the annuitants in the case of an annuity on two lives.

④

This illustration is based on the assumptions set out in the attached personal pension plan illustration which must be read in conjunction with this illustration.

Please see notes

1 This bit of the illustration shows the pension you'd get using the balance of the fund after taking a tax-free lump sum. The pension illustrated here is a level one which will not increase once it's being paid – but you can (and should) usually choose an increasing pension which starts at a lower level and rises each year either by a set amount or in line with inflation. If you are married when you reach pension age, you'll need to decide whether to forego some of your pension in order to provide a widow's or widower's pension to be paid if you die first.   **2** The annuity rate used to convert your retirement fund into pension is laid down under Financial Services Act rules. This is not a guarantee and the rate used when you come to retire could be higher or lower.   **3** Financial Services Act rules say that you must be shown what the pension would be after every fifth year. (The amounts will be the same for a level pension.)   **4** The illustration will be accompanied by explanatory notes, and possibly other literature. **It's important that you read the notes and other material.**

it can investigate your position and advise you on the facts of the case, and it can contact the plan provider on your behalf. You can contact the service through your local Citizens Advice Bureau, or direct (see address on p. 214).

Complain to the regulator

If the firm fails to give you a reasonable response, you should write to the relevant Self-Regulating Organisation, or other regulating body. On one side of paper, if possible, try to summarise the nature of your complaint and the action you've taken so far, including the names and positions of people you've contacted and the relevant dates. The name of the regulating body will be given on the business stationery of the firm. In the case of pension plan providers and specialist financial advisers, the regulating body is likely to be one of the following (see address list on p. 213): Securities and Investments Board (SIB) (members include some building societies – but their deposit-type plans are not covered); Financial Intermediaries, Managers and Brokers Regulatory Association (FIMBRA) (members are many independent investment advisers and managers); Life Assurance and Unit Trust Regulatory Organisation (LAUTRO) (members are life insurance companies, friendly societies and unit trusts – their salespeople and tied agents are also covered.

If you go to a member of one of the following professions: a solicitor, accountant, actuary, or an adviser who is allowed to use the title 'broker', the relevant regulating authority will usually be the relevant Recognised Professional Body (see address list on p. 213): Chartered Association of Certified Accountants; Institute of Actuaries; Institute of Chartered Accountants in England and Wales; Institute of Chartered Accountants in Ireland; Institute of Chartered Accountants of Scotland; Insurance Brokers Registration Council (IBRC); The Law Society; Law Society of Northern Ireland; Law Society of Scotland.

The regulator will either deal with your complaint directly, or, if possible, pass it to a specialised complaints body.

Using an Ombudsman

If your complaint concerns a deposit-type plan issued by a building society and the society's responses have not satisfied you, take your complaint to the Office of the Building Societies Ombudsman (see address on p. 214). The Ombudsman can investigate the complaint on your behalf, conciliate between you and the society and, in the last resort, act as an arbiter in the dispute.

If your complaint concerns a plan covered by the Financial Services Act, you may also have recourse to an Ombudsman or similar scheme. If you've taken your complaint to the regulating body, they will, if appropriate, pass it to the relevant Ombudsman or, in the case of disputes involving a member of FIMBRA, to the Investment Referee. These special complaints bodies will usually try to conciliate informally between you and the investment firm and, if that's not successful, they will act as arbitrators.

The Ombudsmen and the Investment Referee can all specify awards to be made to you, if they are satisfied that your complaint is sound and that compensation is justified. Instead of making a complaint to the regulating body, you could contact the relevant Ombudsman or Referee direct. The Insurance Ombudsman Bureau and Unit Trust Ombudsman (see addresses on p. 214 and p. 215) cover complaints concerning life insurance companies and unit trusts provided they are members of the Ombudsman scheme. The Office of the Investment Referee (see address on p. 214) covers complaints concerning members of FIMBRA. Complaints concerning friendly societies are dealt with by the Registrar of Friendly Societies.

You're not usually bound by the decision of an Ombudsman – if you disagree with it, you can ignore it and go on to take your case to court (see overleaf) if you wish. The decision of an arbiter is binding – so by accepting arbitration, you give up your right to go to court. The Investment Referee can act as an arbiter and, in some cases, so can the Building Society Ombudsman.

At the time of writing, the government has proposed that a special Pensions Ombudsman will be set up who can deal with complaints arising out of alleged maladministration by the managers of a personal pension plan. Details of how to contact the Ombudsman have yet to be announced.

Going to court

If the actions of a plan provider, agent or adviser cause you to lose money, you could try to recover your loss by taking the firm to court and suing them for, say, negligence, misrepresentation, or breach of the Financial Services Act rules. But court cases are generally lengthy and may be costly, so you'd be wise to look on this course of action as a last resort.

Compensation

If your complaint against a plan provider, agent, or adviser is successful and an award is made in your favour – either by the firm itself, through the regulatory or complaints procedure, or by a court – you'll usually recover your money from the firm. But, sometimes, the firm is broke and can't pay up. In this situation, you may qualify for compensation from one of the industry-wide schemes.

If your plan was covered by the Financial Services Act, the Investor Compensation Scheme (ICS) covers the first £30,000 of your investment in full, and nine-tenths of the next £20,000 – in other words, the maximum possible compensation is £48,000. If your complaint was against an insurance company, you may be covered by the Policyholders' Protection Act scheme which covers up to nine-tenths of your entitlement without any cash limit. A claim concerning a deposit-type plan sold by a building society may be covered by the Building Societies Investor Protection Board scheme which covers nine-tenths of your investment up to £20,000 – maximum possible compensation of £18,000.

With the exception of compensation under the Policyholders' Protection Act, the maximum possible amounts of compensation are low compared with the potential size of your pension fund.

Self-defence for shoppers

Though the Financial Services Act provides some very important areas of protection for the investor – and a limited degree of compensation if things do go wrong – no law can stop the really determined fraudster. You should also take your own protective measures:

- do your homework. Work out roughly what your needs are. Read up to give yourself a broad idea of what's available to meet those needs
- have handy the information you'll need – for example, a recent pay slip, forecast of your state pension, booklet for your employer's pension scheme, and so on
- get advice if you need it. With pension problems, solutions are rarely cut and dried, so don't rely on just one adviser – compare the advice of two or three
- don't deal with advisers who are not authorised. With the exception of deposit-type plans (not covered by the Financial Services Act) don't deal with plan providers who are not authorised. Check their status through the SIB Register (see p. 164) *before* you do business with them
- check whether an adviser charges fees. Ask what commissions the adviser will receive.
- avoid salespeople and advisers who don't ask enough questions (see p. 165) – they can't give sound recommendations if they are ignorant of your circumstances
- get everything in writing – for example, make notes of telephone calls, confirm the contents of meetings in a follow-up letter
- read literature and documents. Make sure you understand them before you agree to invest
- avoid paying money to an adviser. Instead, make cheques payable direct to the plan provider – even if you have to write several cheques for different providers.

═══13═══

WHEN YOU RETIRE

Retirement should be a time for relaxing a little, but you may find there's quite a lot of paperwork before you can be sure that your pension income is properly arranged. Here are a few general rules which should help you:

- keep all the documents that you get throughout your working life concerning your pension rights. Don't discard documents relating to your earlier pension schemes and plans
- keep all the papers relating to your pensions in one place – start a file for them, if you haven't one already
- start sorting out your pensions well before your intended retirement date – three to four months before should be adequate in most cases, but allow longer for pensions from any schemes that you left on changing jobs
- always quote relevant reference numbers – for example, your National Insurance number in the case of state pensions, your works number or other scheme reference for an employer's scheme, and your policy or plan number with a personal plan – whenever you contact the DSS, a scheme or a plan provider
- keep copies of letters you send
- make notes of telephone calls – include the date, who you spoke to and the main points of the conversation
- once your pensions start to be paid, keep counterfoils, payslips, and so on, in a handy place. You'll need them when you sort out your tax, and you may want them if you have any queries about your pensions.

It's important that you keep in touch with old pension schemes and plan providers: if you move or change your name, you should contact all the relevant schemes and plan providers to give them your new details. Otherwise, it's all too easy to lose touch, only to find that you have no idea who'll be paying your pension when you retire. At the time of writing, the government is proposing new legislation which will enable the setting up of a registry of employers' pension schemes and personal pension plans which could be used as a tracing service to help people find out the paying authority for their pensions.

Your state pension

How to claim your pension

About four months before you reach the state pension age (60 for women, 65 for men), you should receive a letter from the Department of Social Security (DSS) telling you how much state pension you're entitled to. The pension is *not* paid automatically – you have to claim it, and there should be a claim form (Form BR1) with the letter. Fill this in and return it to the DSS.

If you haven't heard from the DSS within, say, three months before your birthday, get in touch with them yourself by visiting or writing to your local DSS office. You'll find the address in the telephone book under 'Social Security, Department of' or 'Health and Social Security, Department of'. Always quote your National Insurance number on any letters you send, and have a note of it with you if you visit the DSS in person.

Form BR1 asks you on what date you'll be retiring. If you're not yet sure of the date, leave that part of the form blank, but fill in the rest and send it back to the DSS anyway. Let the DSS know as soon as you do have a firm date.

If you haven't claimed your pension in time for your birthday, don't worry. You can still make your claim after reaching state pension age. A pension for yourself can be backdated up to 12 months. But, if you're a man, and you're claiming a pension for your wife based on your own National Insurance (see Chapter 3), the pension for your wife can be backdated only *six* months – so don't delay too long before making your claim.

Postponing your pension

If you decide to put off the start of your state pension (see p. 33), write to the DSS telling them of your decision. When you want your pension to start, contact the DSS and ask for a claim form. This will be form BR46, if you're a man and want the pension to start at age 70, or a woman who wants the pension to start at age 65. If you're younger than this, you'll need Form BR1. You can either contact the DSS office which has previously handled your pension matters, or you can get a claim form from your local DSS office (see p. 185).

How your pension is paid

You can choose to have your pension paid weekly by Order Book, or credited monthly or quarterly to your bank or building society account. If it's paid weekly, you'll be given an Order Book which is rather like a book of cheques already dated and made out to you. You have to nominate a particular branch of the Post Office at which you'll cash your Orders. When you present the Book at the post office branch, they will tear out the Order for the appropriate week, stamp the counterfoil, and give you your pension.

The pay day for weekly retirement pensions is usually Monday. The pension is paid largely in advance as the pension week runs from Sunday to Saturday. You can't cash the Order for a particular week before the date shown on the Order, but you can cash it later provided you're still within three months of the date shown. If for any reason, you haven't cashed an Order within the time limit, contact the DSS.

EXAMPLE

George will be 65 in three months' time but he hasn't had any communication from the DSS about his retirement pension yet – George has moved around a bit during the last 10 years, so it's possible that the DSS don't have his current address. He decides to write to his local DSS office. He looks up the address in the telephone book, and finds it under 'Social Security, Department of, All Enquiries'. His letter reads:

The Retreat,
River Walk,
Wincanton,
Somerset BA9 1PJ

1 July 1990

Retirement Pensions Section,
Department of Social Security,
Federated House,
Hendford,
Yeovil,
Somerset BA22 6SX

National Insurance number: ZB 60 96 24 C

Dear Sir,

Re: retirement pension

I will be 65 on 12 October 1990 and wish to claim my state retirement pension from that date. I've had no communication from the DSS, and I would be grateful if you could send me the appropriate claim form together with details of how much pension I can expect.

Yours faithfully,

George Handy

If you can't get to the post office yourself, someone else can pick up your pension for you as long as you sign the Order (and delete the acknowledgement of receipt). The person collecting your pension must then complete the relevant section on the back of the Order. Only hand your Order Book to someone that you can trust and depend upon, and make sure it is returned to you promptly.

Instead of weekly payment by Order, you can have your pension paid automatically into your personal account (or a joint account that you have with, say, your wife or husband). This can be a bank current or deposit account, a building society savings account, a National Giro current account or a National Savings investment account. Your pension can be credited either four-weekly or thirteen-weekly, and is paid at the end of each four-weekly or quarterly payment period. If you want to have your pension paid direct into your personal account, you should get Leaflet NI105 from the DSS, and complete Form BR436 which is in the back of the leaflet. Having your pension paid into your bank or building society account is certainly very convenient. The drawback is that you receive your pension in arrears.

However your pension is paid, it's important that you let the DSS know if your circumstances change – for example, if you move, marry, become widowed, and so on.

A pension from an employer's scheme

How to claim your pension

Different schemes will have different arrangements but here we give a guide to what you should expect and what action you should take.

About three months before you reach the normal retirement date (or dates) for any employers' schemes that will be paying you a pension, you'll need to be in touch with them. If the schemes haven't contacted you by then, you should make the first move. Either telephone or write to each scheme asking them to give you the details you need and any forms you must complete. If you're not sure who to contact, telephone and ask who deals with pension matters, or failing that you could address any correspondance to 'The Pensions Administrator' and send it to the employer's normal address (or through the internal post system in the case of your current employer). On your letters, always quote any reference number (check your last Benefit Statement for this), and have your reference number to hand if you telephone. It's a good idea to arrange a meeting with the pensions administrator so that you can discuss your position in detail. Don't be afraid to ask for extra information, or advice.

At this stage, you'll need to ask the following questions about the employer's scheme which will be providing your main pension:

- what pension are you entitled to?
- what lump sum are you entitled to?
- will taking a lump sum reduce your pension and, if so, by how much?
- will the pension be increased and, if so, how often and by how much?
- how will the pension be paid; do you have any choices to make about the frequency and method of payment?
- is there a widow's or widower's pension and, if so, how much is it?
- can you increase the widow's or widower's pension and, if so, how will that affect your retirement pension?
- are there pensions for any other dependants, in the event of your death, and, if so, how much are they?

If you've been making additional voluntary contributions, you'll need to know how much has built up in your fund. If you've been paying into your employer's AVC scheme, then they can tell you how much has built up and how you can use it to enhance your benefits from the main scheme. If you've been paying into a free-standing AVC scheme, you'll have to contact the company or society running the scheme as well as the administrators of your employer's scheme.

189

If you're entitled to a preserved pension (see Chapter 8) from a previous employer's scheme, check the documents you have concerning the scheme to find out who you should contact: this may be the old scheme, or it may be an insurance company if, say, the old employer's scheme no longer exists. You'll need to ask what preserved pension you're entitled to, what other benefits there are – if any, what options you have, and how the pension will be paid.

Retiring early

If you retire earlier than the normal age for your employer's scheme you may be able to start receiving a pension even at this earlier date (see Chapter 10). Get in touch with the scheme administrator, relating what you intend. They will advise what pension, if any, you qualify for, and any options you have.

If you're intending to retire early because of ill health, first check the rules of your scheme to see if you might qualify for an ill health pension – you'll probably need to look at the detailed rules (ask the pensions administrator or trustees) since scheme booklets often give insufficient detail. Contact the scheme authorities – *before* your employment stops – to find out what action you'll need to take and what information you'll need to provide. You'll certainly need to provide the scheme with medical evidence – perhaps from the scheme's choice of doctor rather than your own – before a pension can be approved.

Retiring late

Depending on the rules of your employer's scheme, you may be able to put off the start of your pension until after the normal retirement age for the scheme. If you want to do this, contact the scheme administrators, telling them what you intend. Ask them to give you details about how long you can defer the pension, and how it will be increased in the interim.

190

How your pension is paid

Depending on how the pension scheme is arranged, you may get a pension direct from the scheme, or your pension might be provided by an insurance company.

Usually, you'll be able to choose the method of payment which is most convenient for you – for example, a regular cheque through the post or payment direct into a bank or building society account. The scheme rules will generally dictate how often the pension is paid – monthly in advance is common – and when any increases are made.

A pension from a personal plan

How to claim your pension

About three months before you want your pension to start, get in touch with the pension provider, asking for the details you need and any forms that you must complete. If you had previously selected a retirement date, the provider may contact you; otherwise, you should make the first move. Provided you are within the age limits for receiving a pension from your plan (see p. 81), you don't have to actually retire – you can receive a pension but still carry on working.

In any letters, always quote any plan or policy reference number that you've been given. And have the number to hand, if you make contact by telephone.

These are the main questions you need to ask the plan provider:

- how much is your pension fund worth?
- how much pension would the plan provider offer?
- can you arrange for your pension to increase each year, and by how much? By how much will your starting pension be reduced to pay for the later increases?
- what's the maximum lump sum you could have, and how much pension would remain? How much lump sum do you get for each £1 of pension you give up?

- is there a widow's or widower's pension (or pension for another dependant)? How much of your pension must you give up to provide, or increase, a widow's or widower's pension?
- what other options do you have?

When you come to take your pension, you don't usually have to stay with the plan provider with whom you have been saving up until then. Most personal plans include an **open market option** which gives you the right to transfer your pension fund to a different plan provider who will arrange your pension. Pensions can only be paid by an insurance company or a friendly society – so if your earlier saving had been made with a unit trust, building society, or bank (unless you dealt with an insurance subsidiary of the society or bank), you will *have to* switch plan provider at retirement. Some insurance companies choose not to concentrate on the actual payment of pensions; their terms tend to be unattractive compared with companies who do specialise in this area, so it's sensible to shop around at retirement and use your open market option if you find a better deal elsewhere.

If you have protected rights (see Chapter 7) from a contracted-out personal plan, these can – and may have to – be treated quite separately from the rest of your pension. Protected rights can't be paid out until you reach state pension age (65 for men, 60 for women), so you'll have to wait for this part of your pension to start if you retire at an earlier age. You must, by law, have an open market option enabling your protected rights pension to be paid by another provider, if you wish.

How your pension is paid

You can usually choose the most convenient method of payment – for example direct into a bank or building society account, or by cheque through the post.

You may be able to choose whether to have the pension

paid, say, monthly, quarterly or only once a year. The pension may be paid in advance or in arrears. You may get slightly more pension, if it is paid less frequently, since the pension provider can invest your money in the interim.

A very small pension (provided it's not a protected rights pension) may be paid to you as a single lump sum at retirement, instead of being paid as income.

═14═

YOUR TAX IN RETIREMENT

How your pensions are treated for tax

Your state pension

State retirement pensions count as part of your income for tax purposes, and you may have to pay tax if your income is high enough (see p. 196). The exception is the £10 Christmas bonus, which is tax-free.

The pension is paid without any tax having been deducted, which is convenient if you're a non-taxpayer. If you're a basic-rate or higher-rate taxpayer, there will be tax to pay. If you're receiving a pension from elsewhere, or you have a job, the tax on your state pension will usually be deducted from the other pension or your earnings through the Pay-As-You-Earn (PAYE) system. If you don't pay the tax due through PAYE, you'll receive an Assessment from the taxman – usually this will give you 30 days within which to pay the tax.

Employer's scheme pensions

A pension from an employer's scheme is treated as your income for tax purposes, and there will be tax to pay if your income is high enough. Usually, the pension will be paid with tax already deducted through the PAYE system.

PAYE may also be used to collect tax on other parts of your income – for example, tax on your state pension or on income from your investments. This may take you by surprise because it will look as if you're paying too much tax on your employer's pension – see the example on p. 197. If you're in any doubt about the deductions being made, first check your tax position – ask the employer's scheme to help you do this. If you still think you're being over-taxed, contact your tax office.

If, at retirement, you receive a refund of 'excess' additional voluntary contributions (AVCs) – see p. 72 – tax will have been deducted at a special rate of 35 per cent. If you're a non-taxpayer, you can't reclaim the tax. If you're a basic rate taxpayer, you're treated as if you've paid tax on the refund at your normal rate – you can't reclaim any of the tax deducted from your refund. If you're a higher rate taxpayer, you'll have extra tax to pay. The amount you must pay is found by 'grossing up' the net amount of your refund by the basic rate of income tax – this means finding the before-tax amount which would be reduced to the amount of your refund if tax at the basic rate were taken away. Higher-rate tax on the 'grossed up' amount is worked out, but you're deemed to have already paid tax at the basic rate, so your extra tax bill is for the difference between tax at the higher rate and the basic rate – see the example below.

EXAMPLE

Samuel retired in February 1990 and qualified for a refund of 'excess' AVCs at the time he retired. His refund would have been £1,000, but tax at the special rate of 35 per cent was deducted, so Samuel received 65 per cent of £1,000 = £650.

He's a higher-rate taxpayer, so there will be more tax to pay. This is worked out as follows: £650 grossed up at the basic rate of tax (25 per cent in the 1990–91 tax year) is £650/$(1 - 0.25)$ = £867. Tax at the higher rate (40 per cent) would be $0.40 \times £867$ = £347. Samuel is deemed to have already paid tax at the basic rate which would be $0.25 \times £867$ = £217. So he must pay extra tax of £347 − £217 = £130.

Personal pensions

A personal pension counts as your income for tax purposes, so there will be tax to pay if your income is high enough. The pension provider will usually deduct tax through PAYE before handing over the pension to you.

Using the PAYE system, tax on any other income you have – for example, a state pension – may also be deducted from your personal plan before it is paid. This may mislead you into thinking that you're paying too much tax on your personal plan. Before taking any other action, check your full tax position (see below) and the total tax you're paying. If you still find that your tax bill is too high, contact your tax office.

Your tax in retirement

In retirement, your tax bill continues to be worked out in the normal way, but you may benefit from higher tax allowances, so there may be less tax to pay than when you were working even if your income stays the same. The calculations below are carried out for each **tax year**. A tax year runs from 6 April in one year to 5 April in the next. Your tax bill is worked out like this:

- **income** – except for any tax-free income, such as the first £70 interest from a National Savings ordinary account, or the proceeds on maturity from most regular-premium insurance policies – from all sources is added together. This will include your pensions, interest earned by any investments, earnings from any work you do, and so on
- **outgoings** are subtracted from your income. 'Outgoings' is the taxman's name for any expenses you have which qualify for tax relief. These include interest payments on the first £30,000 of any mortgage you have, maintenance payments (within limits) to a former wife or husband, pension contributions if you're still making any, and donations you make to charity under the terms of a covenant. Income less outgoings is called your **total income**

- **allowances** are then subtracted from 'total income'. An allowance is a slice of income on which you don't pay any tax. Everyone (even children) has a personal allowance, and some people – for example, married couples – qualify for extra allowances as well
- what's left is called your **taxable income**. This is divided into two slices. On the first slice (called the **basic rate band**), you pay tax at the basic rate. On anything more, you pay tax at the higher rate. In the 1990–91 tax year, the basic rate band is £20,700, the basic tax rate is 25 per cent, and the higher rate is 40 per cent.

EXAMPLE

Charlotte, who is 66, has the following income in the 1990–91 tax year: state pension of £2,267, employer's pension of £2,200, and income of £3,000 from National Savings Income Bonds. She paid interest of £600 a year on a small mortgage, but had no other outgoings. Her 'total income' was £6,867. She had a tax allowance of £3,670 which left her with taxable income of £3,197. 25 per cent tax on this was £799.25. She received her state pension and her investment income without any tax having been deducted, so the whole of her tax bill was deducted from her employer's pension through the PAYE system. The employer's scheme paid her an after-tax amount of £1,400.75. This made it look as if the employer's pension was being taxed at a rate of 36 per cent (£799.25 tax as a proportion of the employer's pension of £2,200). But, of course, this wasn't really the case, because the tax deducted was the amount due on *all* her taxable income not just the employer's pension.

Bank and building society interest

Note that, until 5 April 1991, you receive bank and building society interest after tax at a special **composite rate** has been deducted. If you're a non-taxpayer, you can't reclaim this tax. If you're a basic rate taxpayer, you are treated as if you have already paid tax at the basic rate. If you're a higher rate taxpayer, there may be extra tax to pay.

In calculating your income for tax purposes, such interest must be 'grossed up' (see p. 195) to find the equivalent amount of income you would have had to receive to have been left with the same after-tax income after deduction of tax at the basic rate. The 'grossed up' amount of interest is used as the basis for calculating the extra tax due from a higher rate taxpayer. The 'grossed up' amount is also the amount which is included in your 'total income' and may thus affect the amount of **age allowance** for which you qualify – see below.

Composite rate tax is to be abolished from 6 April 1991. Non-taxpayers will then be able to receive bank and building society interest without any tax having been deducted.

Your tax allowances in retirement

Everyone has a personal tax allowance. In the 1990–91 tax year, the personal allowance for most people is £3,005. But, if you're aged 64 or over on the first day of the tax year, you qualify for a higher personal allowance called the **age allowance**. In the 1990–91 tax year, age allowance is £3,670 for people aged 64 to 73 at the start of the tax year, and £3,820 for people aged 74 or over.

A husband and wife each get a personal allowance to set against their own income. But they also get an extra allowance called the **married couples' allowance**. This is initially given to the husband, but if he doesn't have enough income to use up the whole married couples' allowance, it can be set against the wife's income. In the 1990–91 tax year, the ordinary married couples' allowance is £1,720. If either husband or wife (or both) are aged 64 or over on the first day of the tax year, a higher married couples' age allowance is payable. In the 1990–91 tax year, the married couples' age allowance is £2,145 where husband or wife was aged 64 to 73 at the start of the year, and £2,185 aged 74 or over.

Age allowances are reduced for people with earnings above a certain level. The personal age allowance is reduced, if you have 'total income' (see p. 196) of more than £12,300 in the 1990–91 tax year. The married couples' age allowance is reduced if the *husband* has income over £12,300 in the 1990–91 tax year. In either case, the allowance is reduced by £1 for every £2 of income above the limit, but the reduction stops once the allowances have fallen to the amounts that people under age 64 receive. In other words, whatever your income, in the 1990–91 tax year, your personal allowance could not be less than £3,005 and the married couple's allowance couldn't be less than £1,720.

The system of tax allowances changed from the start of the 1990–91 tax year. There are special transitional rules which prevent any married couple getting less in allowances than they were getting before 6 April 1990. Single people *can't* get lower allowances under the new system than they were receiving under the old system.

EXAMPLE

Mary and Denis have been married for nearly 40 years. Mary is 66 and qualifies for a personal age allowance of £3,670 in the 1990–91 tax year. Denis is 62. He's too young to get personal age allowance and gets the normal personal allowance of £3,005. But he also receives the married couples' allowance and this is set initially at the higher level of £2,145 because of Mary's age.

Denis, however, hasn't retired yet and earns £12,800 a year – £500 above the £12,300 limit for age allowance. This means that the married couples' age allowance is reduced by £250 (£1 for each £2 of the excess income). Denis' married couples' age allowance becomes £2,145 − £250 = £1,895. This is still more than the normal allowance of £1,720.

Mary's personal age allowance is not affected by Denis' earnings, and her own income is less than the £12,300 limit.

═15═

MAKING YOUR PENSION CHOICE

There are many factors to consider when deciding how best to save for retirement. Which course of action is right for you will depend on your own particular circumstances and, where an employer's scheme is available, on the particular features of that scheme. Here, we pull together the choices you're most likely to face, and summarise the main points to consider in each case.

Employees: should you contract out of SERPS?

1. Advantages of SERPS: the pension is inflation-proofed before and after retirement; the pension is a predictable amount in relation to your pre-retirement earnings.
2. Disadvantages of SERPS: government has reduced pensions for future pensioners and could do so again. If you're young, paying towards SERPS may not give you good value for money.
3. Assuming future investment growth is moderate, women up to the age of 25 and men up to the age of 35 are almost certainly better off contracted out. Women over 40 and men over 50 should almost certainly stay in SERPS or contract back in, unless they are in a good employer's scheme. Between these ages, the choice is less clear.
4. Whatever your age, being contracted-out through an employer's final pay scheme can't reduce your pension compared with staying in SERPS.

5. You can contract out of SERPS without leaving a contracted-in employer's scheme. A rebate-only personal plan is a better route for contracting out than a free-standing additional voluntary contribution scheme.
6. Don't leave a good employer's scheme simply to contract back into SERPS – you'll lose more than you gain.

Employees: employer's scheme or personal plan?

All schemes

1. If the employer's scheme is a non-contributory one, it will be worth joining unless it provides a poor package of benefits. Don't be tempted to think that any benefits are a good thing if you have nothing to pay: joining the employer's scheme will prohibit you from making better pension provision through your own personal plan.
2. Your employer must contribute towards the employer's pension scheme. Would he be prepared to contribute towards your personal plan if you had one?
3. The administration costs per member of the employer's scheme are likely to be significantly lower than the charges set against a personal plan. So, in a money purchase employer's scheme, more of the contributions are left to be invested for your pension and other benefits – and, in some schemes, the employer will meet the costs separately, leaving the whole of the contributions to be invested. (In an employer's final pay scheme your benefits are set independently of the running costs of the scheme.)
4. Your employer probably provides a whole package of benefits: retirement pension, help if you become ill, and help for your family in the event of your death. Would at least some benefits – for example, lump sum life cover – continue if you left the pension scheme? Could you afford to secure comparable benefits through a personal plan? On the other hand, do you need all the benefits? Personal plans let you tailor the benefits to your needs.

5. If you contribute to the employer's scheme, you have to pay in a set amount or a set proportion of your earnings each pay period – monthly, say. Contributing to a personal plan can give you more flexibility over the amount you pay each month.

6. If you leave your employer's scheme now, could you rejoin later if you wanted to?

Final pay schemes

1. If you're within 10 or 20 years of retirement, your employer may be contributing substantially towards your pension through payments to the employer's scheme. Would your employer contribute to your personal plan? If you're young and likely to change jobs a few times, you might not get much benefit from your employer's contributions to the employer's scheme. It won't matter so much, if he won't contribute to your personal plan.

2. If you stay with the employer's scheme for many years, you have the security of knowing that your pension is growing in line with your earnings. This makes final pay schemes particularly attractive if you're an older employee, or if you expect to make a career within one company.

3. You know that your pension will be a predictable proportion of your pre-retirement earnings. This makes it fairly easy for you to judge whether your retirement income is likely to be adequate and to plan extra savings, if necessary.

4. If you change jobs soon after joining the scheme, the benefits might not add up to much. If you expect to change jobs several times, final pay schemes may not be best for you. So, if you're in the early stages of your career, or if you're a woman who expects to take career breaks because of family commitments, a personal plan might be more suitable.

Money purchase schemes

1. Changing jobs shouldn't affect the money purchase pension you've already built up, because the contributions already paid in continue to be invested as before. And, given the other advantages of employer's schemes (see above), joining your employer's money purchase scheme is likely to be a better option than taking out a personal plan.

Running your own company: executive plan or personal plan?

1. In your role as employer, you can pay an unlimited amount into an executive plan (provided you stay within the Inland Revenue benefit limits), whereas there are limits on the contributions paid into a personal plan. So an executive plan may give you more scope for building up a pension fast or providing a wide range of benefits.
2. There's no limit to the benefits from a personal plan (except a cash ceiling on the tax-free lump sum for some old-style plans). There is a limit on the benefits from an executive plan. Once the benefit limits are reached, there's no point making further contributions. For plans taken out on or after 14 March 1989 (or joined on or after 1 June 1989), the benefit limits will be particularly irksome if you earn more than a given cash limit – £64,800 a year for the 1990–91 tax year, increasing with price inflation in future years.
3. The benefit limits – which are defined in terms of your **final pay** – can be a problem, if your earnings fall considerably in the last decade or so before retirement.
4. By varying your employer contributions to an executive plan, you have a flexible tool for helping you to minimise your tax bill. Personal pension plans can also be used in tax planning but to a lesser extent because of the limit on contributions.

Self-employed: old-style plan or new?

1. If you have an old-style plan and you're not using your full contributions limit, you can take out a new-style plan as well. But you'll pay less in charges if you contribute to just one plan.
2. If you're considering giving up your old-style plan in favour of a new-style plan, consider these points:

   - over the age of 35, you can usually make higher contributions to a new-style plan than you can to an old-style plan
   - with a new-style plan you can start to take your pension from age 50; with an old-style plan, you must wait until 60
   - with an old-style plan, you can usually take a larger tax-free lump sum – up to three times the remaining pension. With a new-style plan, you can take only a quarter of the value of your fund. Switching to a new-style plan means you'll have to settle for the lower lump sum. (But bear in mind that if you exercise your open market option under the old-style plan, you'll be bound by the new-style plan limits anyway)
   - you don't have to decide now. You can take a transfer value from your old-style plan at any time before retirement and pay it into a new-style plan. You could even leave this decision until just before you want to start taking a pension.

At retirement: a lump sum from your employer's scheme or personal plan?

1. It's nearly always worthwhile taking the maximum possible lump sum, because the lump sum is tax-free whereas your pension counts as taxable income.
2. You may lose out if you decide to take a lump sum from an employer's scheme which pays pensions that are guaranteed to increase in line with inflation; you'll almost

certainly be worse off if you give up pension from a scheme which tends to inflation-proof pensions even though there's no guarantee. (But with many public sector schemes, you have no choice: you automatically get an index-linked pension and a lump sum.)

3. If taking a lump sum leaves you with less pension than you need, consider using the lump sum to buy a lifetime annuity. This is more tax-efficient than not taking the lump sum at all, because the whole of the pension you give up is treated as income for tax purposes. But part of the 'income' from a purchased life annuity is treated as the return of your original investment and is tax-free; the remainder of the 'income' is taxable. If you run your own business, the main advantages of executive schemes (and SSASs) over personal pension plans (see Chapter 6) are that as the contributing employer, the limit on what you can pay into the scheme is much higher and, to a large extent, you can choose how much you want to contribute each year which gives you a very flexible tax-planning tool. An SSAS also gives you considerable scope to invest in, or lend to, your business, as long as certain conditions are met. On the minus side, the cash limits on benefits which apply to employers' schemes set up on or after 14 March 1989, or joined on or after 1 June 1989, make executive plans less attractive than previously for higher paid people.

GLOSSARY OF PENSIONSPEAK

It's virtually impossible to consider your pension position without stumbling over a vast array of pensions jargon. Some of this has been created by the state as a product of legislation and regulation; some has been created by the pensions industry itself. Unfortunately, not content with just one word for each concept, there are sometimes two or three terms for the same thing. Jargon has its use as a shorthand for long-winded, and sometimes complex, ideas, but it can be daunting for the non-expert. This glossary attempts to enlighten even the most confused. It brings together both the technical terms introduced in this book and other terms that you're likely to come across during your pension planning.

Accrual rate The rate at which you build up pension in a final pay pension scheme. Usually expressed as a fraction of final pay – for example, sixtieths, eightieths or hundredths.

Additional pension Another name for pension from the *State Earnings Related Pension Scheme*.

Additional voluntary contributions (AVCs) Extra contributions you choose to make to boost your pension and other benefits from a particular employer's pension scheme.

Actuary A professional person who is expert at calculating probabilities and future values from available statistical, and other, data. Often employed in the field of pensions and insurance.

Annuity A regular income – for example, paid monthly – which you get in exchange for a lump sum. *Purchased life annuities* provide an income for the rest of your life. You can't get your original capital back as a lump sum. The income from an annuity may be a fixed amount, or it may increase (or decrease). Increasing annuities are generally the most useful form for providing, or supplementing, retirement income.

Annuity rate A way of expressing the amount of income you get from an annuity as a proportion of the lump sum you invest. Where the income from an annuity increases (or decreases), the annuity rate tells you the proportion the starting income bears to the lump sum invested.

Appropriate personal pension A personal pension plan which can be used to contract out of SERPS.

AVC See *additional voluntary contributions*.

Basic pension The main state pension paid at a single flat level regardless of your earnings. If you don't have enough National Insurance contributions to qualify for the full rate, you might qualify for a pension at a reduced rate.

Benefits What you get out of a pension scheme or plan. This may include retirement pension, a lump sum at retirement, widow's and widower's pensions, pensions for children, pensions on retirement through ill health, increases to pensions, and lump sum life insurance.

Benefit statement A regular statement, provided by an employer's pension scheme, showing the pension and other benefits you've built up so far, and what you can expect by the normal retirement age.

Buy out bond Another name for a *Section 32 plan*.

Class 1 contributions National Insurance paid by employees and which count towards the full range of contributory state benefits – for example, basic retirement pension and SERPS pension, sick pay, maternity benefits, and unemployment benefit. Employers also pay Class 1 contributions on behalf of each employee.

Class 2 contributions National Insurance paid by the self-employed. These count towards state retirement pensions and sickness benefit, but they don't count towards sick pay, maternity pay, unemployment benefit or SERPS pensions.

Class 3 contributions National Insurance that you can choose to pay to fill gaps in your National Insurance record for the purpose of qualifying for state basic pension (and widows' benefits).

Class 4 contributions National Insurance paid by the self-employed. They are a straight tax and don't entitle you to any benefits.

Commutation Exchanging part of your pension at retirement for a tax-free lump sum. Inland Revenue rules dictate the maximum lump sum you can have, and this varies according to the type of scheme or plan that you have and when you started to pay into it.

Compound interest   Interest which is added to the original capital sum, and itself grows as interest on the interest is added.

COMPS   Abbreviation for *contracted-out money purchase scheme*.

Contracted-out money purchase scheme   An employer's money purchase pension scheme which must provide a pension at state pension age, and a widow's or widower's pension, which you receive instead of SERPS benefits you would otherwise have got. Your entitlement to these benefits is sometimes called your *protected rights*. The scheme may also aim to provide you with pension and other benefits in excess of your protected rights.

Contracting out   Giving up part of your SERPS pension and getting instead a pension, and other benefits, from an employer's pension scheme or a personal pension plan.

Contributions   What your employer, you, and sometimes the government, pay into a pension scheme or plan. Contributions to the State schemes are called National Insurance contributions.

Deferred pension   Another name for a *preserved pension*.

Deposit administration scheme   Type of pension plan or fund provided by many insurance companies in which your contributions grow by earning interest. Once added, the amount of interest can't be taken away, though future interest rates can change.

Deposit-based pension plan   Type of personal pension plan offered by building societies in which your contributions grow by earning interest. Once added, the amount of interest can't be taken away, though future interest rates can change. Banks can also offer deposit-based plans though, at the time this book went to press, none chose to do so.

Department of Social Security (DSS)   The government department dealing with pensions, among other matters.

DHSS   Abbreviation for Department of Health and Social Security – an old government department which covered pensions, among other matters.

DSS   See *Department of Social Security*.

Dynamisation   The process of increasing previous years' earnings in line with inflation in order to boost the value of final pay used to calculate Inland Revenue limits on pension and other benefits from employers' pension schemes.

Employer's pension scheme   Scheme run by an employer to provide employees with a pension at retirement and, usually, other benefits as well.

Final pay scheme Type of pension scheme in which the retirement pension and some other benefits are related to your pay near retirement (or when you leave the scheme, if this is before retirement) and the number of years for which you've been a member of the scheme.

Free-standing additional voluntary contributions Contributions you choose to make to an AVC plan which is independent of your employer's pension scheme, while still a member of the employer's scheme. The proceeds of the plan must be used to boost the benefits from the employer's scheme.

FSAVC See *free-standing additional voluntary contributions*.

GMP See *guaranteed minimum pension*.

Graduated pension Relatively small earnings-related pension from an old state pension scheme.

Guaranteed minimum pension The amount by which your State Earnings Related Pension Scheme (SERPS) pension is reduced if you are contracted out. Also the minimum amount of pension you receive at retirement from an employer's final pay scheme in respect of periods for which you were contracted out. An employer's final pay scheme must also provide guaranteed minimum pensions for widows and widowers.

Home responsibilities protection Scheme to protect your entitlement to your state pensions while you are caring for someone at home – for example, children or an elderly relative.

Hybrid schemes Employers' pension schemes which work out pensions, and other benefits, on an alternative of final pay and money purchase bases, and give you whichever is the better.

Inflation Sustained increase in price or earnings levels, commonly measured by changes in the Retail Prices Index (price inflation) or changes in the index of National Average Earnings (earnings inflation).

Inland Revenue Government department dealing with, among other things, income tax affairs.

Lower earnings limit Minimum level of earnings set each year to determine the point at which National Insurance starts to be paid, and used in the calculation of entitlement to various benefits. (It is approximately equal to the single person's rate of state basic pension.)

MAPP See *minimum appropriate personal pension*.

Married women's reduced rate contributions A lower rate of Class 1 National Insurance paid by some married women and widows. These contributions do not build up any rights to state pensions.

Middle band earnings Earnings above the *lower earnings limit* and up to the *upper earnings limit*.

Minimum appropriate personal pension (MAPP) Another name for a *rebate-only personal pension plan*.

Money purchase scheme Pension scheme or plan in which the amount of the eventual pension and other benefits depends on the amount contributed, how invested contributions grow, and *annuity rates* at the time of retirement.

NAPF survey An annual survey of employers' pension schemes in the UK carried out for the National Association of Pension Funds.

National Insurance System of contribution payments which entitle you to specific state pensions and other state benefits. The exceptions are Class 4 National Insurance and employers' Class 1 National Insurance on earnings above the *upper earnings limit*, which are straightforward taxes carrying no benefit entitlement at all.

National Insurance Credits Class 1 (or occasionally Class 3) National Insurance that you are deemed to have made, though you have not actually paid them. You are entitled to credits in specified circumstances, such as sickness, unemployment, training and pregnancy. Class 1 credits count as National Insurance only at the minimum level – in other words, as if you had earnings equal to the *lower earnings limit*.

National Insurance rebate Part of your, and your employer's National Insurance which the DSS pays to a Personal Pension Plan, and which must be used to provide *protected rights*. Also the amount by which National Insurance is reduced if you are contracted out through an employer's scheme, and the amount which must be paid into a contracted out money purchase scheme.

Occupational pension scheme Another name for an *employer's pension scheme*.

Pension A regular income, usually paid for life.

Personal pension plan Money purchase type pension scheme run by an insurance company, friendly society, unit trust, building society or bank. It aims to provide you with a pension at retirement and possibly other benefits. A personal plan need not be connected with a specific job.

Plan provider A company, society or other institution which operates personal pension plans. Can be an insurance company, friendly society, unit trust, bank or building society.

Preserved pension The pension you're entitled to receive at retirement from a pension scheme, or plan, to which contributions are no longer being paid.

Rebate-only plan Personal pension plan used to contract out of the *State Earnings Related Pension Scheme (SERPS)*. It accepts only the *National Insurance rebate*, together with basic rate tax relief, and the two per cent incentive, if applicable. These must be used solely to provide *protected rights* when the plan holder reaches *state pension age*.

Retail Prices Index (RPI) Government measure of the average price level in the UK. Changes in the index are commonly used as a measure of price inflation.

Retirement pensions forecasting and advice service Relatively new government computerised service for telling you what is your current, and possible future, entitlement to state pensions.

RPI See *Retail Prices Index*.

Section 32 plan Special plan for receiving transfer values from an employer's pension scheme or a personal pension plan to which you have ceased making contributions. Also called a *buy-out plan*.

Section 226 plan Former name for a *section 620 plan*.

Section 620 plan Old-style personal pension plan superseded from 1 July 1988 by new-style personal pension plans. Can't be used for contracting out of SERPS.

SERPS See *State Earnings Related Pension Scheme*.

State Earnings Related Pension Scheme (SERPS) Part of the state pension scheme which began in 1978 and which pays earnings-related pensions. If you work for an employer, you can be contracted out of this part of the state scheme.

Transfer value Lump sum deemed to have the same value as the pension, and any other benefits, that you are entitled to from a scheme or plan to which you've ceased making contributions. The transfer value is paid into another plan or scheme, subject to some restrictions in respect of *guaranteed minimum pensions* and *protected rights*.

Unitised with-profits plan Pension plan offered by some insurance companies in which your contributions are allocated to a fund whose value is linked to the growth of the company's investments and other factors affecting the company's overall profitability. You also receive bonus units at intervals. The value

211

of your units can't fall, but future increases and bonus units are not guaranteed.

Unit-linked plan Pension plan offered by many insurance companies in which the value of your invested contributions is linked to a specific fund of investments. The value of your plan can go down as well as up.

Unit trust plan Pension plan offered by some unit trusts in which contributions are used to buy a stake (in the form of a number of 'units') in a specific pool of investments. The value of your plan depends on the performance of the underlying investments, and can go down as well as up.

Upper earnings limit Maximum level of earnings set each year, on which employees (but not employers) pay National Insurance. Also used in the calculation of entitlement to the *State Earnings Related Pension Scheme* pension.

With-profits plan Pension plan provided by insurance companies. The return on contributions depends on the performance of the insurance company, reflecting factors such as investment performance, expenses, profit-distribution policy and so on. Your return is in the form of bonuses which are added to your plan at intervals, and when the plan comes to an end. Once added, bonuses can't be taken away.

Working life Officially defined by the state and used to calculate your entitlement to basic pension. For most people it means the tax years from age 16 to just before reaching state pension age – usually 44 years for a woman, and 49 years for a man.

ADDRESSES

Association of British Insurers, Pensions Information Manager
Aldermary House, Queen Street, London EC4N 1TT
Tel: 071-248 4477

Association of Consulting Actuaries
PO Box 144, Norfolk House, Wellesley Road, Croydon,
Surrey CR9 3EB
Tel: 081-668 8040

Chartered Association of Certified Accountants
29 Lincoln's Inn Fields, London WC2A 3EE
Tel: 071-242 6855

Consumers' Association
PO Box 44, Hertford SG14 1SH
Tel: (0992) 589031

**Financial Intermediaries, Managers and Brokers Regulatory
Association (FIMBRA)**
Hertsmere House, Marsh Wall, London E14 9RW
Tel: 071-538 8860

FT Business Publishing
Central House, 27 Park Street, Croydon CR0 1YD
Tel: 081-680 3786

Institute of Actuaries
Staple Inn Hall, High Holborn, London WC1V 7QJ
Tel: 071-242 0106

Institute of Chartered Accountants in England and Wales
PO Box 433, Chartered Accountants' Hall, Moorgate Place,
London EC2P 2BJ
Tel: 071-628 7060

Institute of Chartered Accountants in Ireland
Chartered Accountants' House, 87/89 Pembroke Road, Dublin 4
Tel: 0001 680400

Institute of Chartered Accountants of Scotland
27 Queen Street, Edinburgh EH2 1LA
Tel: 031-255 5673

Insurance Brokers Registration Council (IBRC)
15 St Helen's Place, London EC3A 6DS
Tel: 071-588 4387

Insurance Ombudsman Bureau
31 Southampton Row, London WC1B 5HJ
Tel: 071-242 8613

ISCO5 (DSS)
The Paddock, Frizinghall, Bradford, Yorkshire BD9 4HD
Tel: (0274) 541391

The Law Society
113 Chancery Lane, London WC2A 1PL
Tel: 071-242 1222

Law Society of Northern Ireland
Law Society House, 90–106 Victoria Street, Belfast BT1 3JZ
Tel: (0232) 231614

Law Society of Scotland
Law Society Hall, 26 Drumsheugh Gardens, Edinburgh EH3 7YR
Tel: 031-226 7411

Life Assurance and Unit Trust Regulatory Organisation (LAUTRO)
Centre Point, 103 New Oxford Street, London WC1A 1QH
Tel: 071-379 0444

Occupational Pensions Advisory Service (OPAS)
8a Bloomsbury Square, London WC1A 2LP
Tel: 071-831 5511 (weekdays, 10 a.m. to 4 p.m.)

Office of the Building Societies Ombudsman
Grosvenor Gardens House, 35–37 Grosvenor Gardens,
London SW1X 7AW
Tel: 071-931 0044

Office of the Investment Referee
Centre Point, 103 New Oxford Street, London WC1A 1PT
Tel: 071-379 0601

RPFA Unit
Room 37D, Central Office, Newcastle-upon-Tyne NE98 1YX

Securities and Investments Board (SIB)
3 Royal Exchange Buildings, London EC3V 3NL
Tel: 071-283 2474

SIB Register enquiries
Tel: 071-929 3652

Society of Pension Consultants
Ludgate House, Ludgate Circus, London EC4A 2AB
Tel: 071-353 1688

United Trade Press Ltd
PO Box 54, Laindon, Basildon, Essex SS15 6SS
Tel: (0268) 410181

Unit Trust Ombudsman
31 Southampton Row, London WC1B 5HJ
Tel: 071-242 8613

INDEX